IS IT E

Darian Leader is a ~~...~~ ..lyst and the author of many book ~~...~~ .cluding *The New Black* and *What is Madness?* He practises psychoanalysis in London, and he is a founding member of the Centre for Freudian Analysis and Research, and a member of the College of Psychoanalysts, UK.

By the same author

Introducing Lacan (with Judy Groves)
Why Do Women Write More Letters Than They Post?
Promises Lovers Make When It Gets Late
Freud's Footnotes
Stealing the Mona Lisa: What Art Stops Us from Seeing
Why Do People Get Ill? (with David Corfield)
The New Black: Mourning, Melancholia and Depression
What is Madness?
Strictly Bipolar
Hands
Why Can't We Sleep?
Jouissance: Sexuality, Suffering and Satisfaction
Rereading Little Hans

IS IT EVER JUST SEX?

Darian Leader

PENGUIN BOOKS

PENGUIN BOOKS

UK | USA | Canada | Ireland | Australia
India | New Zealand | South Africa

Penguin Books is part of the Penguin Random House group of companies
whose addresses can be found at global.penguinrandomhouse.com.

Penguin Random House UK,
One Embassy Gardens, 8 Viaduct Gardens,
London SW11 7BW

penguin.co.uk
global.penguinrandomhouse.com

First published by Hamish Hamilton 2023
Published in Penguin Books 2024

001

Typeset by Jouve (UK), Milton Keynes
Printed and bound in Great Britain by Clays Ltd, Elcograf S.p.A.

The authorized representative in the EEA is Penguin Random House Ireland,
Morrison Chambers, 32 Nassau Street, Dublin D02 YH68

A CIP catalogue record for this book is available from the British Library

ISBN: 978-0-241-99816-8

Penguin Random House is committed to a
sustainable future for our business, our readers
and our planet. This book is made from Forest
Stewardship Council® certified paper.

A City trader would set himself the same target each month, much higher than what his boss expected of him, and almost always succeed in meeting it, despite the volatility of markets and financial recession. When he didn't, he'd go online to hook-up apps, arranging a drink and then sex with an unknown woman. He'd make the same small talk during the drink and run through the same motions during the sex: hydraulic penetration with little foreplay, ejaculation and then a swift, insensitive departure. During the sex, he'd avoid eye contact and think of the profit that he'd failed to achieve with his trading. Back home, he'd take a Xanax and fall asleep, with no thought for the person he'd just been with.

We might ask here, why was the sex necessary? Was it, like the Xanax, simply a way of self-medicating, of calming anxiety and the acute sense of unease that accompanied his failure to control the markets? Was it a hidden attempt to communicate with another human being that just short-circuited each time, or perhaps a hostile act that he was unaware of? When I asked him about the number itself, the figure that he felt duty-bound to generate each month, he explained that this had been the highest profit of a star trader in his previous company. This was the number that he felt compelled to achieve ever since, and nothing less was acceptable.

The sex acts that took place when he failed could thus hardly be taken as expressions of some basic sexual instinct but, on the contrary, as treatments of his failure to be equal – in some sense – to another man. This, of course, could be interpreted sexually – was there a desire or jealousy between them? – but his heterosexual act was clearly an acting-out, where sex was filling some other, less obvious function. The repetitive unchanging nature of the sequence suggested that the identity of the woman was unimportant to him, and that something else was being played out each time, something that looked like sex but was never just that.

This might seem like a kind of strange reversal of psychoanalysis. Analysis was once famous for seeing sex in everything: physical and psychical symptoms were explained in terms of unconscious sexual desires, and it meant that if you met an analyst at a drinks party you had to be careful what you said. Sex was the unspoken secret of just about everything, shaping both personal relations and the wider social dramas of war, politics and culture. Yet, as the American critic Kenneth Burke asked in the 1930s, what if sex itself were the cover for other, even more important motivations? If men, for example, are said to think about sex every seven seconds, are they actually thinking about something else, or indeed, could thinking about sex be a diversion from other, less palatable thoughts?

Later research claimed that the seven seconds was more like once every one and a half hours, and, more generally, that thoughts about food

3

were just as or even more significant. This obviously depended on where the person was in their life – a baby, an adolescent, a senior – and on a host of other factors, but it raises the question of what we are really thinking about when we think about sex. Everyone knows that with food, it's rarely just about food: we eat or think about eating when we are unhappy, uneasy, agitated, anxious or lonely. Does the same apply to sex?

The global use of internet pornography surges late on Sunday night and continues through Monday, the day when most people return to work, and so presumably have to face problems and pressures that the weekend shielded them from. Porn use at the office, indeed, clocks in at 63 per cent of male and 36 per cent of female workers. The appeal to sexual imagery here might well be analgesic, and research on sexuality in the twentieth century has only compounded this question, suggesting that humans don't really have an innate sexual instinct that aims at copulation. Bodies aren't like sticks that make fire when you rub them together, since so many conditions, preferences and cues are necessary for us to even become aroused.

The frequent comparisons of our sex lives with those of animals — they're doing it like rabbits — are unhelpful here, as animal behaviour is not always as automatic and instinctive as we might imagine. If sheep can have sex in the first few days of life, male chimps may need months or even years of practice to be able to function sexually, just as male apes have a steep learning curve. A long period of sharing a cage can make sex less likely, and preferences and even sexual styles may stop some species from indiscriminate coitus. The old idea that sexuality is a smouldering animalistic force within us, desperate for release yet restrained by social forces, has little to support it, and even what looks like excessive mating behaviour might be a measure of frustration rather than sexual drive.

Biologists and ethologists had already argued in the 1940s and 50s that if most of the lower mammals have sexual instincts governed by hormones, this is not the case for us, and that even the expression of hormones can be inhibited or arrested by psychological factors, to delay puberty or interfere with sexual maturation. What pushes us to seek sex is far more complicated than some endogenous motor, resulting more from social processes than from innate biological ones. What these processes might be is one of the things that I will explore in this book, together with the more general question of what place sex might have in our lives and, crucially, what we are actually doing when we are doing sex.

Scientific studies of sex that seek an explanation here by hooking people up to a measuring apparatus while they watch blue movies or copulate tend to disappoint, as they neglect the dimension of *meaning*, so central to human interactions. If we experience penetration, for example, as an act of possession or love or exploitation, that gives it a meaning, which is difficult to then ignore or negate. When people say, 'It was just sex, it didn't mean anything,' this just shows how important meaning is to the whole process, yet meaning is difficult, even impossible, to measure.

It is easier, of course, to count orgasms, and scientific studies and pornography thus share the same approach: they both divorce sex from meaning, and from the question of loyalties that arguably define human attachments. In porn, after all, the characters never show any loyalty to anyone: they don't turn down sex due to prior commitments, just as in scientific experiments subjects are not included if they decline to perform. All the recent projects to create an emancipated pornography – what we could call 'parity porn' – seem oblivious to this, when all it takes would be characters who say 'Not now' or 'Not you'.

The hook-up culture of hit-and-run sex that the internet has facilitated so widely in recent years encourages users to make their sexual activity like porn or like a scientific study: simple physical operations on the convex and concave surfaces of a human body. Yet the pain, heartache, regret and sense of emptiness that accompany the highs of excitement show that much more is at stake. What people desire sexually and what they actually do when they meet someone else are usually wildly different, with the margin between them occupied by phantasy. How do our phantasies form and what effects do they have on sexual life?

And if most people's sexual lives begin with phantasy, what can prepare us for the eventual collision of bodies? Why are arousal and satisfaction so rarely commensurate? What does it mean to be penetrated, and why do we not only penetrate but press, caress and mouth other bodies? Why do we apply pressure to skin and muscle? Why do we bite, scratch and squeeze? In surveys of sexual behaviour, no human society has been found in which violence is absent from sexual relations, and their vocabulary is shared. The word 'force' is the single most common verb to describe sexual acts, and the language of domination, possession and conquest is ubiquitous.

Even the great sexual handbooks of the East like the *Kama Sutra* describe sex as a form of combat, detailing the varying patterns of assault and defence, the angle and positioning of striking fists and the variety of marks left on the body by nails and teeth. Nail marks are classified into categories such as 'crescent-shaped', 'circular', 'lotus' and 'tiger's claw', with teeth marks described as 'elephant tusk', 'broken cloud', 'boar's bite' or 'line of jewels'. Each party is encouraged to respond to violence with violence, but lovers are instructed to be sensitive to injury as during their excitement they may lose awareness of the severity of their blows.

The early sex researchers found the place of pain here difficult to rationalize. In the States, when Alfred Kinsey and his colleagues published their pioneering works on male and female sexuality in the late 1940s and early 50s, many of the interviewees found sex 'disgusting', 'nasty', 'revolting', 'brutish', 'painful', 'exhausting' and 'unsatisfying'. And when William Masters and Virginia Johnson explored sexual activity in the 1960s, the thousands of women they spoke to experienced pain during sex in almost every case, yet only three had felt able to ask their partner to be more gentle, and not a single one had told them to stop.

Today, although it might seem as if everything has changed, there is still a real stigma around voicing discomfort and pain in sex, especially for women. This is not just about hurting a lover's feelings, as there may be a real risk of provoking further violence, a daily reality for probably the majority of women in the world today. Between a quarter and a half of women in countries with data on this report having been physically abused by a present or former partner. The fact that many instances of violence are not reported – or cannot be – suggests that even these shocking statistics are in fact underestimates.

In analytic practice, I continually meet adults who have never had sex except when drunk, as if the bodily activities, processes and sense of threat are just too disturbing to bear without anaesthesia, even if the partner is perceived as caring and considerate. Although it is sometimes said that sex is all about communication, it is surely the one part of our lives where we are in fact least likely to communicate what we are really feeling and thinking. So, if we have a choice, why do we do it?

*

Children ask exactly the same question. Sex is puzzling, nonsensical, anxiety-provoking and impossible. Did one body really go inside another body? How can that happen? Didn't it cause damage? How could anyone find that pleasurable? And how do bodies survive sex? These questions might just seem like the products of naivety and lack of information, but they continue to haunt us throughout our lives, sometimes consciously and probably always unconsciously. They might even shape what we actually do when we have sex, as we will see later on.

The first thing to notice here is how these childhood questions create a link between sex and violence. Penetrating a body means breaching its boundaries, just as the act of childbirth involves a tearing or cutting of the body surface. One of the first questions that children ask about sexuality is a very simple one: where do I come from? How was I made? Regardless of the sanitized answers they receive, certain equations tend to be made, using other areas of the child's experience, to create what Freud called the 'sexual theories' of childhood. Just as the body's excrements derive from what we eat and drink, so too a baby may be equated with a bodily product that results from ingestion.

In her study of children's ideas about the origin of babies, Anne Bernstein found that this theory was in fact much more complex. An initial belief that babies have always existed would later become the problem of how they were manufactured: so the first dilemma was to explain their whereabouts, and then the recipe. For some children, the baby had always been there inside the mother or grew in her like a seed; for others it was made outside her and then inserted, either fully formed or like a perfect miniature. When we blame religion and patriarchy as the sole causes of pro-life campaigning and legislation – as the recent overturning of Roe v. Wade has so dramatically highlighted – it is worth considering whether these infantile theories may also play a part in the passions ignited.

In one of Bernstein's examples, after a mother explained the biological realities of sex and conception to her son, he walked away muttering, 'But I know she really swallows it.' Babies must be created through some kind of oral process, deriving ultimately from what we put into our bodies since swallowing is the most familiar route to the stomach. And hence the child's idea of a baby made of food that exits anally, although, as the little boy's comment suggests, there may be an idea of some other kind of swallowing at play here too, perhaps of a miniature baby or of the father's sex organ or seed. The anus is privileged here as it provides a much more obvious image of a pathway out of the body than a vagina, re-inforced by parental scrutiny of the child's excretory acts. Entry and exit tend to follow an oral–anal template, as both parents and children worry if what went in has managed to come out.

Freud and later infant researchers argued that the idea of an abdominal rather than an anal exit would come to replace or co-exist alongside of these earlier theories, and was just as or even more frequent. Indeed, the idea of a food-baby being pooed out could even be seen as a defence against the more disturbing underlying image of birth as a bodily mutilation. Children as old as twelve still believed that birth involved a baby being cut out of the mother's belly with some sort of knife, a bloody and terrifying operation that clashed with cosy ideas of maternity and loving a cherished baby. The belly button is often a puzzling and fascinating object for young children, identified as the site of this violent exit. It can be tugged, probed and investigated endlessly, with adult explanations deemed unsatisfactory.

If so many female children are socialized from an early age to imagine a future role as mothers and carers, these unpalatable and frightening thoughts are difficult to accept. How can their parents wish such a future upon them? The bloody images of bodily fracture may be swiftly repressed, but the curiosity that follows may contain its own violence. We tend to think of children's curiosity as a wonderful quality to be celebrated, but it also means taking things to pieces, breaking objects apart, cutting up dolls and even dismantling living things like insects to see what's inside.

Perhaps surprisingly, little boys also think of themselves as potential mothers. Even if they know that men don't give birth bodily, they may have archaic fears of a baby or small animal bursting or gnawing its way out of them, as we learn from working with young children. In adults, the phenomenon of couvade is well known, in which a man mimics the pregnancy symptoms of a woman – such as nausea, vomiting, abdominal swelling, leg cramps – and one study even found that men imagine that their own body has got smaller after their female partners gave birth. The biblical story of the birth of Eve from Adam's rib echoes this, with its image of both an abdominal exit and male pregnancy.

This has been explained in different ways: an initial identification with the mother – who is usually in such close proximity to her child – means that the boy's body is undifferentiated; the wish to be her or to be like her; or a basic lack of understanding of sexual differences. Both boys and girls may also harbour a desire to give the mother a child as a way of creating a distance from her, of no longer being her exclusive object themselves. Whatever the case, the horrifying image of a violent abdominal exit is quite pervasive even in the adult imagination, as we see in the popularity of the *Alien* movies in which the monstrous creature tears open a hole in the stomachs of its hosts.

This link of sex to violence, danger and pain here is escalated when we realize that a baby only got there in the first place through a sexual act. One's very existence means that something unthinkable must have happened. However enlightened the parents and however intelligent and worldly the child, a connection is created here between sex and reproduction that, at some level, can never be broken. As the writer Nora Ephron put it, describing her own understanding of sex, 'It had never crossed my mind that sex had anything to do with desire or bodies or that you did it except when you wanted to have a kid.' Whatever information we absorb later on about pleasure and non-reproductive sex, it may be impossible to completely 'unlearn' this primary piece of learning.

Adults, indeed, often treat their children's questions about sex as questions about babies, as this makes them less uncomfortable, and they conflate the issues together, as well as the anatomy. The vagina and the uterus are rarely differentiated, and qualities of the one are frequently applied to the other. As for the clitoris, its relevance to pleasure rather than reproduction can be the very reason for its exclusion: 'It's easier to talk about the vagina because it's a reproductive organ,' a mother explained, 'but telling my daughter about her clitoris seems like telling her to go masturbate.' It used to be joked that the only people who understand that sex and reproduction are not the same thing are anthropologists and adolescents, but perhaps all of us equate them, regardless of our knowledge of biology, our use of contraception and our desires and wishes.

We can all laugh when a child with one sibling who has just learnt the facts of life asks its parents in a shocked tone, 'So you had sex twice?', but the connection may be enduring. Every time we have sex, the thought of conception may be present consciously or not, and it may even be separated from the reality of the sexual act. I have heard teenage and adult patients several times explain how they fear they might be pregnant even if they have never had sex. College-educated people in positions of great social responsibility can say 'I know it sounds crazy but I am sure I am pregnant' in the full knowledge that this is a biological impossibility.

The obvious interpretation is that the fear is just a wish, but in many cases the way we learn about sex in early childhood spreads out to include a much wider field. Even if we are told that the baby exits the vagina, any bodily aperture may become a potential exit site, just as any substance taken into the body may become an initiator of pregnancy. Being socialized to not think about the genitals only reinforces this, as now the qualities of the genitals must be ascribed to other areas of the body. Vaccines are especially significant here, as the idea of a 'shot' is frequently the only available image of a bodily penetration for children.

Therapists in the last few years were often startled to find that educated adult patients declined the COVID vaccine for exactly this reason: 'I know it's absurd, but I just feel that the injection going into my body might make me pregnant.' While the media paid more attention to anxieties that the vaccine might compromise or interrupt pregnancies, therapists were also hearing an inverted narrative: the vaccine itself would fertilize.

Adult decisions and choices were being shaped

here by childhood beliefs and phantasies, and we should never underestimate their power. Such ideas are rarely talked about as they seem so absurd, yet are they any more so than the common thought patterns labelled OCD, where someone may feel that if they don't touch a door handle a certain number of times a loved one may die? Religious culture of course reinforces such patterns, with stories of virgin birth and miraculous conception, and these may become overarching frameworks of our understanding of biology itself.

When we then turn to the sex act that results in babies, the stakes are just as high, and factual explanations often have little effect. After Ephron's mother completed her sex education by telling her that 'Daddy puts his penis into Mommy's vagina', she knew very well that this was 'not an explanation about sex at all', and it left open all the consequences and conditions that a child's mind can think of. To imagine oneself as the potential bearer of a child implies that one will be a sexual object open to penetration, a realization that can only render bodily anxieties even more acute. If the anus is the most obvious image of a pathway or aperture, this means that a lifelong fear – perhaps combined with a wish – of anal penetration will be established. The odd biological fact that the anus and lower bowel are so densely innervated can be experienced as a disturbing reminder of this, and jokes, folklore and popular culture continually play on these anxieties.

During sex, the handling and kneading of the female buttocks tend to be considered a justifiable excitant, but a het man, even if highly aroused, will rarely be able to admit to this same desire (unless he pays for the privilege of disclosure to a prostitute or a psychoanalyst). At a cultural level, one's whole being can be equated with this part of the body, as people refer to themselves and others as 'my ass' or 'your ass'. I am always puzzled when visiting the States at this conflict of contractions and expansions: instead of saying that a store is at the corner of 'Orange Street and Hicks Street', people say 'Orange and Hicks', and yet, in the same breath, they can say, 'I'm going to take my ass down to the store.'

*

Freud was struck here by what he called the 'sadistic' notion of coitus, and the child's 'obscure urges to do something violent, to press in, to knock to pieces, to tear open a hole somewhere'. In his discussion of the five-year-old Little Hans, he described the boy's idea of sex as 'smashing something, of making an opening into something, of forcing a way into an enclosed space'. Freud's account uncannily echoes Baudelaire's threat to Madame Sabatier in his *Flowers of Evil* to 'make in your astonished flank, a wide and gaping wound ... and through these new lips, more bright, more beautiful, infuse my venom into you, my sister'.

How else, indeed, could a child imagine the act of penetration without this imagery of breaching and breaking? And the danger of Baudelaire's 'venom' is echoed in the once common verb for being made pregnant: 'poisoned'. LGBTQ+ activist and writer Amber Hollibaugh remembers finding a set of xeroxed illustrations of sexual positions when she was ten and studying them with her friends in a field behind her home, 'desperately trying to understand how anyone could enjoy doing what those pictures suggested'. Comparing the images with their own bodies, they wondered how a penis could actually enter inside them: 'I got sick. I threw up for fifteen minutes. Sex and penetration were horrifying ideas.'

Yet beyond this primary and terrifying sense of discrepancy – how could it fit? – Freud thought that the earliest ideas of violent sex happen before the child even recognizes the existence of a vagina. It's not a penis entering a vagina but something tearing into a bodily space, left unclear and undefined; less an aperture that facilitates penetration than the actual creation of a hole. No surprise then that the sex play of children so often involves the apposition of the genitals without any actual attempt at penetration. The act of love, he wrote, is seen as an act of violence, and so the sexual activity of the future becomes not a promise but a threat. To borrow Andrea Dworkin's description of male sexuality, this is 'the stuff of murder, not of love'.

Many of Freud's students disagreed with this explanation, arguing that children were perfectly aware right from the start about anatomical difference, and that the disappearance of the vagina was in reality a later defensive reaction. This would be rather like the old instruction to hotel staff to say 'Excuse me, sir' if ever they intruded upon a woman bathing. The misattribution is there precisely because the reality has been perceived. Faced with the dreadful thought of a penis entering a vagina, with the pain and damage this would no doubt inflict, it was natural to deny its existence. But what exactly was being denied? How could a child have anything like an accurate knowledge of this internal space that was so difficult to picture or represent except by analogy? And hence the appeal of the many children's stories about hidden spaces enclosed within other spaces: passageways, corridors and rooms that had to be discovered; magical openings in a rock; the sudden appearance of a concealed door; secret nooks and hideaways that are still so fascinating for adults.

Note how these hidden spaces are almost invariably linked to both safety and danger. They represent a special refuge for the girl, a place she can seek solace and distance from family and friends, yet at a certain moment others learn about them and they are no longer safe spaces. What was once a containing perimeter becomes the site of potential invasion, and girls now often start to voice fears of burglars and intruders. The bodily symbolism tends to be quite clear here, with anxiety around entry through doors and windows translating the fear that bodily apertures will be breached.

An analysand described her memory of these feelings on seeing the Jodie Foster film *Panic Room*, in which a mother and child hide from intruders in a specially built concrete enclosure concealed in their home: 'There it was, the secret room I'd always dreamt about, the place where I could hide, but where those bad men were desperate to find me and harm me.' The recent *Escape Room* franchise makes this danger even more acute, where it is the containing space itself that will kill you unless you can get out fast, and many cities now have actual escape-room spaces where office parties pay to solve puzzles that will enable their exit.

If early perceptions of the vagina are often

forgotten or repressed, they may be rediscovered later on, a narrative that resonates both with infant research and what we learn from some child and adult patients. Vaginal sensations felt in adolescence or adulthood can spark an extraordinary sense of déjà vu, as if a much earlier experience were suddenly being accessed once again. The remarkable number of girls' stories concerned with refinding a hidden treasure or the restoration of some lost item have usually been interpreted in a phallic way – she refinds the penis she once had and believes had been lost – but note how the rediscovery is often of a wondrous hidden door or opening, suggesting a reconnection with an area of vaginal sensation that had been radically muted or, as the psychoanalyst Selma Fraiberg put it, 'sealed off' by a fear of penetration or of overwhelming internal excitement.

These early experiences of the body do not presuppose an actual knowledge of the vagina, and this continues to elude most adults, even gynaecologists, as Masters observed when he first began his research into sexuality. Its patterns of expanding and shrinking only compound this mystery, and it is difficult to ascribe a single image to the vagina that would account for these changes. If bodily products make the inside more tangible, how can we tell what shape it is unless we use a baby or poo or penis shape as our template? And how does this invisible body part become part of the body?

Whether we agree with Freud here that there is an initial ignorance of the vagina or with his students that there is a sensory awareness, both perspectives imply that a body will be torn open, and it is important to recognize that this violence is at play for everyone concerned. According to some cross-cultural work, there is no documented society in which violence during consensual sex is unilateral: it is always reciprocal. Lovers may bite each other savagely, spit at each other, and tear out chunks of each other's hair and even eyebrows. Adult men in Western cultures often imagine splitting open a women's body while having sex – which they describe as arousing – and sometimes also feel guilt afterwards at damage caused.

In their groundbreaking work comparing human and animal sexual behaviour, using Yale

University's databank on the sexual habits of 190 documented societies, Clellan Ford and Frank Beach concluded that if the existence of a sexual instinct aiming at penetrative sex was not evidenced, the one thing that was sure was the link between sexual excitement and the infliction of pain. This has seemed more basic than even efforts at reproduction, and the famous title of the Sharon Stone–Michael Douglas film exploring the links between sex and danger – *Basic Instinct* – while ostensibly referring to sex at the same time denoted homicide.

We could think here of all the unfortunate verbs that men put at the end of their boasts 'I fucked her till she . . .', indexing the collapse or destruction of the female body. Sexual achievement and harm converge, as if both the aim and the condition of arousal involved suffering. Canadian sex researcher and therapist Claude Crépault reports the case of a judge who would phantasize while having sex with his wife about a woman's terror that he would light the fuse of the dynamite he had inserted in her vagina: he would only be able to come at the moment of her most intense panic.

This is one of the reasons for the success of medical scams in countries which rely on insurance systems. After a sexual encounter, someone claiming to be a doctor phones the male party and says that the female party has been genitally damaged during the sex act, and a transfer of funds for urgent treatment is required. The panic and guilt that the man feels may block a rational assessment of the situation, and the money gets sent. Penetration and damage are on a continuum here. Women are not targeted in these scams, yet may feel concern not that they have caused palpable damage to the man's body but sometimes that they may have contaminated him.

The fear of harming the other person can be so great that sex is avoided altogether, and the relatively recent efforts in many societies to make men more sensitive to the wishes of women in sexual situations reinforces this. Terrified of a predatory and threatening sexuality in themselves, some men prefer to steer clear of sexual relationships. However, the majority tend to insulate themselves from such thoughts and continue to practise a largely violent and coercive sexuality, in which the attempts to break open a body described by Freud often hold centre stage.

Outrage and anger at sexual crimes reported in the media is one of the ways such insulation works. The aggressive attacks are projected outside the self, yet the sympathy for victims may mask an enjoyment of their plight. When the journalist Kate Webb was eventually released after being held captive for several weeks by the People's Army of Vietnam in 1971, she noted how everyone seemed disappointed that she hadn't been raped. Men, especially, are continually searching for stories of assault on women as a way of keeping their own violence at the right distance. Even in the midst of a crucial Brexit debate in July 2018 that would change the country's future, the most clicked-on story in the UK press was not about the political negotiations but about a woman who had apparently asked a man to tie her up and beat her.

The job of the media, in part, has been – and still is – a curation of violence against women, usually masquerading as concern. In sex itself, even if the man seems to be loving and tender, he

may only be able to sustain an erection by imagining forcing his way into his partner. And in
their cars, male drivers tend to get upset at any
hindrance to their forward motion, making jokes
about scoring points by running over an elderly
person. As the historian of sexuality Gershon
Legman observed, the victim is always a little old
lady and never a little old man, just as the female
murder victims in TV shows and movies vastly
outnumber the dead men.

*

Freud had very little to say about rape – beyond
an unfortunate footnote in which he endorses
the view that a woman may unconsciously welcome
the assault – and, as many writers of second-wave
feminism pointed out, would at times construe sex
as an act with one active and one passive party. It
is remarkable to see here how much of the
important early work on this question has been
largely airbrushed out of histories of the
women's movement. The standard divisions
between first- and second-wave feminism tend

to eclipse the work of women writers and activists in the 1940s and early 50s. Ruth Herschberger's 1948 book, *Adam's Rib,* is arguably the single most significant work of the twentieth century on women's subjectivities and gender, yet today at the time of writing there is not even a Wikipedia page for her.

This brilliant, dazzling work explores gender stereotyping, how medicine and biology ignore the reality of women's bodies, how benchmarks of male sexuality suppress the complex models of female desire, how male narratives rewrite the reproductive process, and how gendered active and passive splits characterize so much of sexual life. Simone de Beauvoir almost certainly read it during her stay in Chicago the year before submitting *The Second Sex* for publication, and readers who remember the book's appearance say they were just stunned by it. Herschberger herself was so affected by the intensity of the book's reception that she chose never to publish another work of non-fiction in her lifetime, focusing instead on writing poetry.

Herschberger starts by challenging the male

myth that any application of pressure to an erogenous zone will produce an experience of pleasure, a
bias that underwrites justifications of sexual violence and that stories the woman as ultimately
willing when a man touches her. Male activity
here is understood in terms of a terror of intimacy,
and an avoidance of the fact that female desire is
not some unipolar force but switches from recep-
tive to propulsive in a cyclical way. The idea of
motherhood annulling sexual desire is decon-
structed, and Herschberger discusses desire after
the menopause, questioning the male periodizing
of the female lifespan. Crucially, she explores how
male notions of sexuality always aim to animate
one portion of the sexual encounter and de-
animate the other, mapping this on to the gender
split of male–female, to reinforce the idea of active
men and passive women.

Herschberger was alert to the way that language
shapes our thinking here, and questioned why
people referred to female 'frigidity' and male 'impo-
tence' rather than the other way round – which had
once been the case historically – and how 'erection'
was applied to the 'penis' and 'congestion' to the

clitoris and vaginal tissue when the process of engorgement was ostensibly identical. She argued that a more complex vocabulary was needed to talk about sex, one that avoided binary logic and that recognized the 'minute and complex degrees between pleasure and non-pleasure'.

As to the question of violence, Herschberger described how caregivers socialize children in very different ways, not just through what they say and the social ideals they transmit but through how they touch. She distinguished the 'pressure contacts' on skin and muscle, and how for the girl these were scripted to change with marriage and the sexual acts this involved. It was now the male set of pressure contacts that mattered, as if it were no longer a woman's choice, with the assumption that these contacts would automatically generate arousal. Her chapter on 'The Rape Myth' shows how these beliefs about excitement reinforced the active–passive paradigm and the cultural conceit that the 'essence' of masculinity is the impulse to penetrate.

The evolutionary narratives that posit some innate male violence to forcefully acquire females in Neolithic times only reinforce these tropes, and implicitly frame male violence as somehow natural. Interestingly, so many origin stories involve a primary act of violence, from myths about the creation of the universe to stories about the founding of human societies: there is always some Big Bang or transgressive homicidal act. The idea of an ancient hard-wired male urge to penetrate females obviously also has the implication that females have an ancient hard-wired urge to be penetrated. So more justifications for a misogynistic status quo.

Rather than seeing children's perceptions of sex and birth as violent acts as the precipitates of this Neolithic heritage, Freud's arguments suggest that the notion of a Neolithic heritage is itself a phantasy product of these perceptions. We imagine our origins as violent acts. This is not to deny the weight of history and patriarchy, as these cultural forces clearly shape how we interpret the present, the past and the future, and push adults to socialize male and female children in gendered ways, tending to prime boys for aggression, physical achievement and acts of possession.

Developing this early work on the gendered dynamics of sex, Shulamith Firestone argued in *The Dialectic of Sex* that the violence Freud saw in the child's conception of sex might have been a phantasy but one that was probably rooted in the reality of the family situation, in which a mother suffered violence, bullying and humiliation from a father – a point which Freud in fact makes himself in his essay on the sexual theories of childhood. Many other writers agreed that hetero penetrative sex actually was an act of violence, and so in a way the child's phantasies were perfectly correct. This presupposed, of course, a version of sex in which a man aggressively penetrated a woman, perpetuating the warped power differential which had for so long been the hallmark of patriarchies, and which waterbeds did little to modify.

What writers like Herschberger and Firestone showed so clearly was that sex was being taken as a given, even if the forces that acted upon it were not. This was the problem with much of the early psychoanalytic approach to sex, with its idea that we are punished for sex rather than by means of it. The emphasis on the repressive forces of society operating on humans' vital sexuality often obscured the forces at play within it. Religion and popular culture only reinforced this bias, as youngsters in horror movies are inevitably killed savagely while they are making out, just as many aspects of religious culture condemn sex outside marital and reproductive frameworks: sex is wrong until certain conditions are fulfilled.

These cultural forces are so strong that when youngsters watch horror movies today and see a couple about to have sex, they immediately understand that this is the prelude to their death. The characters who avoid sex tend to survive, while those who engage in bodily pleasure get killed. All this in our enlightened times, showing that however much sex education and surface morality may have changed, sex is still at some level considered a punishable offence. Indeed, when people gossip about sex, their talk is invariably full of moral rather than just physical vocabulary: 'I can't believe she/he/they did that! What a . . .'

Judgement is at a premium here, with men and women divided subtly or not so subtly into good and bad, and evaluations functioning to whitewash those who are making them. As Joan Nestle put it, where curiosity builds bridges, judgement builds the power of some over others. Yet what we risk losing sight of here is that if sex must be punished, it may in itself involve forms of punishment: when the young couple making out in the horror movie are skewered with a metal spear by some mass murderer, we forget that perhaps their making out actually involved one skewering the other with a penis. So one kind of violence obscures – or justifies – another.

Freud did not develop his initial observations on the sadistic theory of coitus and on the anxieties and terrors at the risk of a breach of bodily boundaries. And yet even before the question of sexual penetration becomes thinkable for a child, there is surely the very pressing concern, 'What is the edge of me?' Bodily holes and invaginations are endlessly explored in the second and third year of life, together with their edible correlates: doughnuts, pretzels, bagels, macaroni. It is always a significant moment when children start to draw closed curves and bounded shapes, and show an interest in keeping things like clothes and stationery apart and separate. This may correspond to the effort to mark out body edges: we feel more secure when a boundary can be maintained, as in the safety evoked by urban police doing their 'rounds'. Loops need to be closed and gaps avoided.

This is made all the more urgent by the negativity ascribed to exudations like urine, shit, sweat, spit and blood which break bodily boundaries. As parents express their displeasure or revulsion or concern at these aspects of the body, they effectively colonize them, leaving the traces of their own judgements on the child's body. When these substances exit the body, they must be removed or hidden, but even when they remain inside they may become the focus of anxiety: what will happen if too much wee or poo builds up? Will I burst? What can I do to stop this from happening?

These bodily substances that can be both inside and outside are usually tabooed in some way, and so become the source of both threat and fascination. Underarm sweat, for example, is often considered today as somehow offensive and in need of suppression, yet in the late nineteenth century could be wiped on fingers or a handkerchief and presented as a romantic overture. Children, likewise, can be enthralled by their own bodily fluids, yet feel disgust when finding them unexpectedly. What our parents say about these bodily leavings can still echo in our minds throughout our lives, and habits and ceremonials tend to be constructed quite early on around them that rarely change. The question of the body's edges thus becomes even more complex, as they include both 'me' and the judgemental gaze of parents.

When this question of boundaries becomes linked to sex, coitus can hardly be understood as a pleasant or natural act. Too much is at stake, and the integrity of the body is at risk. And indeed, in folklore and mythology, the penis is almost universally depicted as a weapon rather than an instrument of pleasure, just as the vagina is represented as threatening or as some sort of trap. If this is how we first learn about sex, why on earth would we be so drawn to it later on, and how could it possibly come to embody the most meaningful of all human activities? Could sex just be the only avenue of violence permissible to many of us in our adult lives?

As an analysand put it, 'I have sex with my boyfriend in an angry way. It's the only place where I feel permitted to express anger, although he doesn't notice.'

*

These childhood phantasies and beliefs about sexuality are being forged in a very strange place. Parents tend to avoid directly answering questions about sex, and often fail to label or simply mislabel body parts and processes. A child might be admonished for some bodily activity without being told why it is wrong, and so various injunctions are transmitted in an opaque and nonsensical way. Touching one's genitals is punished or discouraged without a clear reason — usually well before the child can even speak — and so an atmosphere of negative judgement is created around that part of the body.

Parents, indeed, often require an almost complete censorship of the genitals apart from their role as excreting devices. Children are taught to avoid thinking about their sexual organs, and must learn how and when they can refer to or touch them, with special lexicons and confusing misattributions. The term 'vagina' is often used to evoke the vulva, and the clitoris tends to be excluded altogether. Having a body means learning to be suspicious of it, and, as the psychologist Seymour Fisher pointed out, the body image itself is a kind of coded submission to parental rules, values and taboos.

Even as recently as 2019, almost half the population of the UK lacked a basic knowledge of female genital anatomy, showing how the taboo here is still widespread, despite the most enlightened sex education. Almost 60 per cent of men and 45 per cent of women could not label the vagina, with even less knowledge about what the urethra was and where the labia are. Older research had shown how men think that the vaginal entrance is about 4 inches higher than it is in reality, and many people find it extremely difficult just to look closely at their genitals. The vagina is often imagined by boys as a neat round hole like the anus, and there is widespread ignorance in both sexes of the positioning and shape of the hymen.

Psychoanalysts themselves are not immune to this, and although some of the first medically trained analysts would actually conduct a genital examination of their patients, interest in the sexed body would swiftly become peripheral. Judith Kestenberg once asked if analysts were even aware of the existence of the prostate gland, despite its significance for sexual and urinary life. Freud would have to visit the bathroom during analytic sessions, and it would be very difficult, Kestenberg observed, to find a patient whose father did not suffer from prostate issues, yet psychoanalysis behaves as if it simply doesn't exist. When Freud's patients wrote memoirs of their experience of analysis, they could evoke some brilliant interpretation he made, but not whether it happened before or after he had come back from peeing.

Even more curiously, when the prostate does appear in popular discourse it is totally desexualized, despite the vital function it has in supplying components of male semen and the secretions and sensations that may disturb boys in early childhood. A patient described problems he was having in his relationship due to his massively increased demand for sex, and when I queried this, he explained that he needed to have sex every day to ward off the risk of prostate cancer. When I googled the research, it turned out that cancer risk is reduced by a staggering 31 to 36 per cent if males over fifty ejaculate at least seven times a week, with two to three times offering far less protection. Yet while other results showing that some medication, lifestyle or dietary change can reduce cancer risk by 10 per cent will make media headlines, the prostate statistics seem to have been almost totally blanked, as if the link between prostate health and sexuality was just not thinkable.

For many children, the only discourse around the genitals concerns whether they are clean or not, and so an equation is established between sex and hygiene which may stay with them for the rest of their lives. Most people, in fact, wash their hands after rather than before peeing, so that rather than protecting their genitals from germs they are protecting themselves and other people from potential defilement. Childhood words for the genitals associate them more frequently with pooing or peeing than with spatial analogies (a jewel box, a sausage), as if this is their primary function, and a very significant percentage of women – at least 25 per cent – avoid cervical screening and other gynaecological consultations because they are worried that their genitals will be perceived as dirty.

Both men and women may shy away from sexual activity for the same reasons, worried that their genitals will appear unclean or unsavoury in some way. It is no accident that jokes about sex, indeed, are called 'dirty' jokes, perpetuating the association between dirt and sex, and the more that public discourse beyond the family tells us not to feel guilty about sex, the more that personal hygiene becomes paramount, as if it is perhaps proportional to the surface devaluation of guilt. The less guilty we're told to be, the more we keep scrubbing and spraying!

The weight of parental judgement is heavy here, and children swiftly learn that curiosity about sex risks parental disapproval. And so, as Gershon Legman pointed out, perhaps the real sexual enlightenment of the child is not learning how babies are made but understanding that an interest in sex can mean rejection and punishment from those whose love we need. This can be a devastating discovery, and reinforces the muting of genital sensations, and their ascription to other parts of the body. Children's ubiquitous 'tummy aches' are sometimes in reality states of sexual excitation that have gravitated away from their source and lack the possibility of vocalization.

Similarly, parental comments on sex tend to be about what not to do, what to avoid and what is somehow wrong or sinful, despite our enlightened and information-savvy times. Even the most liberal parents tend to forbid boy–girl sleepovers, as if the prospect of the two sexes cohabiting the same space is just too dangerous, even if they know full well, perhaps from their own childhoods, that same-sex sleepovers almost inevitably involve opportunities for sexual contact. The paradoxes of parental disapproval and validation here show the difficulty in dealing with sexuality and recognizing its effects.

The violence played out in childhood games is another example of this. If children play at killing each other, no one objects, but if they play at sex this is almost always admonished, as if even homicide is more acceptable. When kids' comics were first mass-marketed in the late 1930s, images of scantily dressed women being tortured were swiftly censored: more clothing was added to the women's bodies but the torture left untouched, as if violence perhaps had a censoring quality in itself. Damage to a body stood for – and in the place of – sex.

In Margaret Atwood's short story 'Murder in the Dark', children play the classic game, folding up pieces of paper and mixing them up in a hat or bowl. Whoever picks the scrap with an 'X' on it becomes the detective and temporarily leaves the room, while the person who gets the black spot becomes the murderer. The lights go out, and the murderer selects their prey, either whispering, 'You're dead,' or putting their hands round the victim's throat. Atwood starts the story by telling us who is in love with whom, turning the darkened space into a sexual scene, where 'the excitement was almost more than we could bear', and the feigned murder clearly takes the place of a forbidden sexual act.

These transformations and censorships of sexual imagery result in a strange segregation. The genitals become partitioned off from the rest of the body, and the unease in speaking about them means that they now occupy a clandestine space, a special site which the parents have some superior knowledge of and which in some senses they retain psychological possession over. Four- and five-year-old children, indeed, in one study classed the area above the knee and below the navel as 'not me'. This segregation is echoed in the way that genitals are often given proper names, as if they had an identity separate from that of the child, and several popular works of literature from the thirteenth century onwards feature talking genitals, according them an identity and autonomy distinct from the rest of the body.

The split between the child and their sexual

body parts tends to take place in a climate of negativity, judgement and secrecy. Secrecy here is not just about hiding but about being alone. Parents so often ask their children what they were doing when they have been away or on their own, as if separation in itself means that something illicit, or beyond parental control, may have occurred. Even in later life, many adults feel the urge to masturbate the moment they are alone, as if aloneness creates a condition for sexual arousal, rather than the other way around. Entering a public space, the person may then feel that others can tell they have been doing something wrong, even if they recognize how irrational the thought is.

When parents focus not just on the child's relation to their own body but warn them of potential dangers in the outside world, things get even more complicated. If the first thing the child hears about sexuality concerns fear of attack, this may then become part of desire, as if the idea of something dangerous, illicit and forbidden occurring is linked to that of an external predator. Early writers in the women's movement lamented that parental concern for the basic safety of their female children from an invasive and threatening male world risked having the consequence that arousal and threat became soldered together.

*

In their groundbreaking and still unsurpassed 1973 study of sexuality, John Gagnon and William Simon argued that these aspects of parent–child interaction are less a sanctioning of sexuality than the actual creation of sexuality. It's not that there is some original sexual drive that is being curbed by the parents and by society but that sexuality is itself the contradictory, uneven space where we feel a negative judgement together with both too much and too little meaning, a meaning that is largely created and conditioned by the sense of judgement. It's less that some bodily activity has sexual meaning but that there is no meaning except that created by the sense of judgement.

Anything that comes into this space can then take on a sexual value, especially if it has some link to the body. So anything secret or that we feel we have to hide or that seems unexplainable becomes potentially sexual, just as anything that is forbidden or negatively judged can generate sexual desire. Parental language here tends to be moral – 'dirty', 'bad', 'wrong' – and this moral value then shapes sexual meaning. This implies, as Gagnon and Simon argue, that learning about sexuality is essentially learning about guilt, and that managing sexuality is managing guilt. No surprise then that so many people become unwell around sex or develop symptoms that block the accomplishment of sexual acts.

The very intensity of sexual feelings and acts, they suggest, may be the result of this atmosphere of guilt and anxiety. We mislocate the source of this intensity to our bodily, physiological states, when in fact it is being shaped by worries and concerns that largely escape our conscious awareness as adults. Several studies from the 1930s onwards had shown how infants and children display the physical signs of arousal – erection, genital engorgement, lubrication – at times of fear, anger, anxiety and other charged moments, yet all this will be forgotten by around age twelve. Triggers for erection included: getting one's school report, being late for school, watching a war movie, being chased by police, finding money, being punished, seeing one's name in print, being angry at another boy, watching marching soldiers, and falling from a garage roof.

Early studies at Yale had shown how baby boys will erect when frustrated and restless, and Kinsey even thought that all emotional situations produce erection in boys prior to adolescence, when codings for the right socio-sexual cues are more solidly internalized. It is well known, indeed, that schoolboys often have to hide erections when getting off the bus in the morning, and erections can be produced by accidents, near-accidents and fear of punishment. Similarly, while some researchers sought the source of vaginal lubrication in glandular secretions, others argued that the physiology was comparable to that of sweating in situations of acute anxiety and fear. In one case, a woman trapped in a car wreck during an accident experienced her first orgasm, and this would then become the material of her masturbation phantasies.

It is important here to differentiate arousal from what a person is perceived to 'want' at a conscious level. If a woman lubricates vaginally in a situation of threat and panic, this doesn't mean that what she wants is threat and panic, a mistaken assumption that has been used tragically to discount claims of sexual assault and rape. Agency here is not a simple effect of physiological change, and cannot be directly inferred from it. After Roxane Gay was betrayed by her boyfriend and then gang-raped at age twelve, she describes how for years 'unless I thought of him I felt nothing at all while having sex', and that 'when I did think of him the pleasure was so intense it was breathtaking'. This does not mean that she wanted to think of him, or that she wanted to only to be able to experience pleasure when she did so.

An Auschwitz survivor told me that what had shocked her the most on arriving at the camp were not the horrific living conditions and imminent threat of death but the way in which women masturbated quite openly on breaks from their work detail. Nothing was hidden, nothing had to be explained, it just happened right there before her unbelieving eyes, as if the sexual activity was there not as an expression of pleasure or communication but as a basic response to terror.

Bereaved people, indeed, may be horrified to experience intense sexual desire directly after a loss, and the link of arousal to disorienting and frightening situations may seem bizarre. When the clergyman Laud Humphreys carried out the field research for his study on sex in public toilets, he found himself trapped with a small group of other men as a gang of violent homophobes besieged the building. They had to brace themselves against the door to stop the incursion, and bottles and stones were thrown through every window. Yet during this time of acute threat and danger, as they did everything they could to maintain their barricade, Humphreys was baffled to see how acts of fellatio continued to take place. Writing about his experience later on, he found this 'impossible to understand' unless sexual excitation was understood as in some sense an effect – or a treatment – of their perilous situation.

Studies of sexual arousal that had initially

assumed it would be conditioned by positive emotions and situations came to shift their emphasis: by the 1970s it was widely recognized that fear, anxiety, anger and grief could all generate sexual feelings, even the sight of someone being mutilated and killed. Ovid had observed centuries earlier that bloody gladiatorial games were the perfect setting for the start of sexual liaisons, and soldiers in the First World War trenches reported intense states of sexual arousal preparing for an attack. Excitement, it seemed, needed a dose of risk and even terror. The old belief that anxiety and threat would block sexual arousal and performance was effectively reversed.

Psychoanalysts were embarrassed to find that even a direct threat to someone's manhood could help sustain rather than inhibit erection. In one unusual study, men who were threatened with knives were able to have sex when one might have thought that the menace of castration would have blocked them. Of course, this turned out to be slightly more complicated, as those who had prior difficulties maintaining erection were made worse by anxiety, whereas only those without manifest 'performance' issues found their sexuality enhanced. Just as significant as these measures of arousal were the accompanying disturbances of memory: children tended to have erased memories of physical arousal by their teens, and parents who were asked to report on the signs of sexual excitement in their kids would forget what they had documented after only a two-week period.

These relations between fear, excitement and hostility have been studied for many years in many different contexts. It has been claimed that hostility can energize sexual desire, and that sexual desire can energize hostility. Or that both aggression and sexuality are just derivatives of some basic and non-specific force within us. Or that we just misconstrue the feelings of anger, hostility or anxiety we experience as sexual arousal, given that the basic physiology is more or less the same. However we interpret the results of these studies and experiments, it is clear that excitement and fear are very closely intertwined, although we may not always be able to make meaningful distinctions between them.

An escort described her regular visits to a

High Court judge, where he would instruct her to disrobe and act out the alleged crimes of the case he was currently hearing. This was clearly both a necessary and a helpful supplement for him, and the interactions never involved intercourse, although he would masturbate after the role play. One might guess that these encounters were what allowed the judge to lessen his own anxiety around his cases, and perhaps to be able to process his own artificial position of authority. The escort expressed concern that her acting abilities might affect his actual judgement of the cases, and so she would be in some sense responsible for errors in sentencing. Sex here is both a result and a treatment of anxiety, and also perhaps for an unconscious sense of guilt.

The rise in porn use during the pandemic can at one level be linked to the fact that access to social spaces was compromised, to working from home, and, as some have argued, to boredom, but it surely also reflects this presence of anxiety. Porn here did not just mean the previously available categories but the rapid appropriation of a whole new repertoire of features. As early as

March 2020, more than 1.8 million searches for coronavirus-themed porn were logged by Pornhub, featuring sex with masks, surgical gloves and even hazmat suits. The signs of infection and prevention had been almost instantaneously appropriated to serve as indexes of arousal and licences for intimacy rather than distance. Threat was converted here into a source of excitation.

This proximity was often quite undisguised in the mainstream porn cinema of the 1970s. In *The Story of Joanna*, the male protagonist shares his thoughts about death, mortality and meaninglessness before the sex gets going, and the blockbuster *The Devil in Miss Jones* – grossing almost as much as that year's Bond film – is actually a porn adaptation of Jean-Paul Sartre's play *No Exit*, famous for its slogan 'Hell is other people'. The film opens with the main character cutting her wrists and dying, before returning to Earth as the embodiment of Lust. Sexual excitement here is depicted as either a treatment or an exploration of human finitude and despair, and existential themes were at a premium.

Just as we may be unaware of our existential

questions, so arousal itself is often opaque to us. Adults can experience genital engorgement without any conscious feeling of excitement, and most studies here show a rather low correlation between perceived and physical arousal. The more that the sexual stimuli are deemed culturally taboo – rape, practices labelled as 'deviant' – the greater the gap between how excited the body is actually getting and how excited the person will think themself to be. Men will admit to enjoying images of women in pain when they think that they have been drinking alcohol (in fact placebo from the experimenters) yet deny this otherwise, and how they quantify their own arousal can be deftly manipulated by providing false feedback: if they think (wrongly) that their heart rate is increasing, they claim to be more aroused by erotic imagery.

Lubrication, likewise, can occur without a woman's knowledge, just as the penis can have various kinds of erections in both its distal and proximal portions with no accompanying sense of excitation. Erection, ejaculation and orgasm do not always occur together, as teenagers discover, often to their surprise: ejaculation can happen without an erection, just as orgasm does not necessarily depend on either ejaculation or erection, as Kinsey had emphasized. It is well known that soldiers under fire can ejaculate without any kind of erection, and Magnus Hirschfeld reported the case of a man at the front who ejaculated on simply receiving a letter from home. Even penile detumescence is quite variable in young men, and some escorts – who have a choice – prohibit under twenties, not due to any shadow of incest but simply because the lull after ejaculation may be absent and the sexual demands are consequently excessive.

Physiological reaction here has no automatic link to satisfaction. In one bizarre study, women doing an arithmetic task showed more signs of labial stimulation than those listening to a sex scene from *Lady Chatterley's Lover*, and increased heart rate, respiration or lubrication tend not to correlate with any set increases in pleasure. These signs of bodily arousal may in fact be accompanied by a sense of unease or unhappiness, and, as we've seen, are not obviously distinguishable from the experience of anxiety. Such processes may be transitory or sustained, and show how sexuality here is not only outside our voluntary control but also often outside our conscious awareness.

Few people, indeed, may be aware of a feeling of hostility during or just prior to sexual arousal, but a great deal of research on excitation has found that it has a central role. We see this not only in the acts of physical violence which form part of sex – pressing, pinching, squeezing, biting – but in the often very conscious feelings of aversion or disdain felt afterwards towards the partner. These seem sometimes to just come out of nowhere, but they may well form part of the background of the arousal itself, in the same way that arguments in a couple are often a prelude to sex. Similarly, if a job interview panel seem inexplicably hostile, it may be that the spikiness conceals a sexual desire towards the applicant.

The presence of such desires in a family is generally unthinkable, yet is no doubt a part of the reason why fathers sometimes turn away from their daughters as they hit puberty. A close, caring relationship may dissolve into distance and estrangement, as the father blanks out the sexual feelings in himself, and now suddenly loses interest in his daughter's studies and may withdraw both encouragement and material support. Baffled by this behaviour, the daughter may in turn play out dramas with friends and lovers in which a reproach is levelled at someone who is punished for their apparent indifference.

*

We see this complex relation between guilt, anxiety and desire at a cultural level. If a particular society or social space like a church or a boarding school privileges a specific taboo, the outlawed act may come to represent someone's desire, even if they have no intrinsic interest in it. The cultural taboo is less imposed on the wish than the wish is shaped by the taboo. In England we often hear it said that all public schoolboys are repressed gay people, but what this actually means is that the more a school system makes same-sex attraction ostensibly taboo, the more that images of gay desire will appear in dreams and phantasies to represent desire.

This is not to say that same-sex desires are simply the product of taboos but that whatever is strongly prohibited can take on a symbolic, erotic value, including, of course, heterosexual desire, as Freud's theory of the Oedipus complex suggests. Sexuality initially has no determinate content, but is created in the atmosphere of negative judgement, secrecy and prohibition that comes from without, and which can be applied to any form of attraction. Anything that takes on these qualities can then become equivalent to desire, and this may shift historically, as what was a sexual crime in one era becomes a sexual variant in another.

Despite all the social changes over the last century, however, the way that desire is represented culturally is always quite close to crime, and while homosexuality was itself criminalized, it often functioned as one of the only available images of sexual desire. In today's media, sexual lust tends to become visible when a boundary is crossed: an affair, a betrayal, an act of exploitation, an assault. When heterosexist norms are in place, desire is usually tempered by an association with love, marriage and babies. Newspapers and feeds report celebrity couples forming, but the power of sexual desire to create these unions is given less emphasis, until it emerges as the force that breaks up the couple later on. Desire inhabits this space of negativity and transgression.

Food and eating can easily enter this compact. If a family is particularly focused on food, with multiple rules governing what can be eaten and when, a margin opens up to represent what escapes the system. Eating against the rules can then become a vital part of a child's life, even if food has no special appeal in itself. Similarly, if a child grows up in an atmosphere in which any wish is deemed excessive, and they are expected to be purely passive recipients of parental commands, what space can there be for the child to actually want anything? Any desire is automatically condemned as desiring *too much*.

This means that the moment that something becomes wanted, it will seem to the child to be in itself excessive, with the admonishment and guilt that goes with it. Any asking becomes the internal question, 'Am I asking too much?' Desire then might only be able to emerge in fleeting moments of 'too muchness', in the form of what one might even want least of all: what one finds most repulsive or disgusting. Since wanting is not permitted, desire becomes reduced to something that looks very different, something beyond 'wanting', often using taboos as a springboard since what is prohibited takes on the quality of 'too much'.

And this will then create cycles of guilt and shame, as both the very fact of wanting and the actions that embody a beyond to this (like bingeing or allowing detritus to build up around one) are experienced as unacceptable and wrong. We find a similar dynamic in some cases of so-called 'sex addiction'. As therapist Jack Morin points out, sex 'addicts' are often less hooked on sex than on fighting with it. Desires that are based on taboos and prohibitions will escalate in tandem with the need to resist them, generating cycles where the battle with desire seems more powerful than the actual pull of the object of desire. Sometimes it seems as if the sexual object is less another human body than guilt itself.

Pornography also relies on the presence of taboos to create arousal, and at multiple levels: the taboo on the medium itself, and the taboos on the acts represented within it. Kinship relations are violated (incest porn), professional boundaries broken (sex during medical or tradesperson visits) or class divisions overridden (servants and domestic workers as sexual objects). In the mid 1990s, half of all downloads depicted bestiality, incest or paedophilia, with less than 5 per cent showing vaginal sex. In 2016, 'mum', 'step-mum' and 'step-sister' were among the top ten rubrics searched for on Pornhub, and during the pandemic the new category of 'COVID porn' relied on the breach of health protocols. Today, with massive increases in online porn use, incest and assault porn are virtually unavoidable, and children and young people are frequently traumatized by exposure to this.

The only traditionally non-taboo aspect of sexual life seems totally absent: a wife and husband having sex. To claim DIY porn as a counterexample, where couples post their own sexual videos online, is still taboo-breaking, in the very fact of the public posting. Surface taboos on debasement are also of course broken, as amateur porn contains more gender inequality at women's expense than industry-created porn. As Gagnon and Simon formulate the rule of porn, if the activity is conventional, the context is not; if the context is conventional, the activity is not.

But is that all there is to human desire? If prohibition can at times forge attraction, there are surely other kinds of desire, or other inflections of it, that steer our lives. When we read about the gynaecologist who sees genitals all day but can only become aroused when peeking in a public toilet, is it simply the prohibition that explains the excitement? Psychoanalytic thinking has been quite split on this point. The traditional view was that the unconscious is made up of quite concrete wishes – to possess the mother, to replace the father, to be everything for the mother, to win the father's love, etc. – most of which are outlawed by the incest taboo, and hence come to embody desire.

But later work totally shifted this. The content of the unconscious was not wishes but neglect and deprivation: how our parents and caregivers had failed us, how they had not been there when we needed them, leaving a hole in our psyches that we then tried to fill with the concrete desires that the first generation of analysts had focused on. Desire was thus in itself a defence, a way out, that gave us a direction and kept the abyss of parental absence and failure at bay. And this was taken to explain why the exit from a depression is so often the emergence of a desire, be it romantic or professional. And also, perhaps, why what seems to be the satisfaction of desire in sex might leave us feeling empty and unfulfilled afterwards: it was only a temporary stopgap for a deeper, more fundamental absence.

An analysand described how, on a trip with her family, she had visited a toy shop. This was an unusual experience and she was initially thrilled to be there, yet as she wandered around the store she felt the increasingly powerful need to 'want to desire something'. The day before she had been struck by how the group of people they were with had all seemed to have things to do, to have goals and aims: to want things. Yet now she was in exactly the kind of space in which a wish would be granted, yet there was just no wish. 'What I wanted the most, more than anything actually there, was to want something.' Desire here was not a primary foundational urge but more like a compass point that she searched for.

Complicating this a little bit more is the fact that desire and sexual excitation are not exactly the same thing. We tend to think of desire as a vector, a single linear force, being pushed or pulled in one particular direction. But excitement, as Robert Stoller argued, is bidirectional, 'a dialectic, a rapid oscillation between two possibilities (and their affects). One we tell ourselves has a positive, the other a negative outcome: pleasure/pain, relief/trauma, success/failure, danger/safety. Between the two lies risk.' There is a movement between the expectation of danger and the avoidance of danger. This more complex description surely echoes the realities of sexual experience, and the contradictions that we find there, as Roxane Gay showed so clearly in her account of how trauma and excitement had been fused. Linear views of desire simplify this, and seem to do away with the tensions and paradoxes that characterize arousal, and it is a very real question how human beings manage the friction between desire and excitation when they become involved in an actual sexual encounter.

*

So what happens when we meet real-life flesh-and-blood partners? How could the preferences and orientations developed in infancy and childhood possibly prepare us for the strange experience of sex? And especially given the terrible anxieties about bodily boundaries that we discussed earlier. If it is true that our sexual lives tend to start with phantasies – about sex, birth, reproduction – do we just try to adapt the realities we knock up against to our own private scenarios? This seems undeniable, as we repeat the same situations in our sexual practices over and over again, yet, as Gagnon and Simon pointed out many years ago, the idea of a fixed phantasy template fails to factor in how sexualities can change and how they may be, to some extent, moulded by social forces.

In place of the traditional concept of phantasy

they introduced what they called 'sexual scripts'. A script is like a code, directing what we think and feel and how we act, and it is composed of three basic dimensions: cultural, interpersonal and intrapsychic. If we have spent years phantasizing about a particular person, and then, away on a trip, we return to our hotel room to find them there naked waiting for us, we are more likely to call the police than to become sexually aroused. This is because the right script is not being followed: for someone to be perceived as sexually available requires a lot of coding, a lot of situational and psychological cues that we learn as we grow up. It is never about a brute animalistic response of a body to a body, even if this is what we like to think that sex is about.

Even when very young children play sex games with each other, they start out with social roles – 'You be the doctor, I'll be the patient' – as if sexual exploration requires a minimal script, a basic positioning of places for anything to happen. These places are almost inevitably highly gendered – often using the active–passive template – but it is worth noticing how often children are eager to switch roles: 'Now I'll be the doctor and you be the patient.' The way we inhabit these roles may become more fixed as we grow older, but the script is always there, with the different codes encrypted within it. These scripts, as Gagnon and Simon observed, are basically strategies for managing guilt.

Cultural codes tell us broadly what we can do, with whom and where, and establish sequences in sexual relations: certain people may be ruled out as sexual partners and others admitted, just as kissing may be the first step in a sexual encounter in some cultures but seen as bizarre in others. When Ford and Beach conducted their survey of the sexual habits of 190 societies, they found that what was taken for granted in the US might seem utterly nonsensical and repellent in other parts of the world. Some cultures excluded mouthing nipples from sex whereas others placed a high value on this. Some encouraged reciprocal violence, others condemned this. Some privileged sudden inhaling of the partner through the face, others foreclosed any notion of nasal aspiration.

Even what were understood as erogenous

zones could be shaped culturally. Certain parts of the body with abundant nerve endings were usually taken to form 'natural' areas of sensuality, but there was actually no immediate correspondence between nerve distribution and erotic value. In the mid 1970s, for example, popular sex culture was filled with references to male nipple arousal, and it was widely depicted and described in both visual and print media. People sexually active at that time remember how this became a part of sex, yet within less than a decade it had fallen off the agenda. Sex acts involving a man were less bound to include nipple stroking and mouthing, even if some people may of course have retained the practice.

We see the same phenomenon today with acts of asphyxiation. Although choking has been part of some people's sexual repertoire for hundreds of years, it is pervasive today, especially with young people. Often explained solely in terms of violence against women, it is a more complex activity, as there are a higher number of self-inflicted fatalities than deaths by misadventure. Both men and women die every year through self-asphyxiation in masturbation ('scarfing') – 90 per cent men – and this has been documented for the last fifty years. But it has now become a much more common part of sexual behaviour, showing again how an erotic practice can be shaped and facilitated by social forces.

Even the noises we make during sex may be culturally conditioned. It might seem obvious that the sounds we utter in the heat of excitement are involuntary, but the selection of words and noises we produce varies historically, and can also depend on religious background and social class. Some people invoke the deity as they cry out 'Christ!' or 'God!', but others steer clear of these expressions. Similarly, during the seventeenth century it was common for people making love to clap their hands at moments of intense pleasure, whereas today this would probably be seen as a weird turn-off.

Socio-economic class is also a major force here in shaping what scripts allow and disallow. We might think that a childhood relation to a parent would ultimately dictate what we do in bed – so if we were breastfed, for example, we might eroticize the nipple or sucking actions – but this can only be part of the story since sexual practices have turned out to be so dependent on class. Kinsey and his colleagues were surprised to see that the frequency of oral–genital contact and breast mouthing was pretty much predicted by whether the person had more or less than nine years of formal schooling, even if today, in the age of message multipliers like the internet, these traditional stratifications of sexual activity are less pervasive.

Scripts also tell us where we can have sex, although of course when certain places are ruled out they may for that very reason become eroticized (the broom cupboard at Nobu for Boris Becker). Most people in the world today share a room with more than just their immediate partner, and privileged Western standards of bedroom privacy are both a current and a historical exception. Interestingly, trains were once highly sexualized spaces, and in Joseph Weckerle's extraordinary catalogue of the 531 sexual positions possible for human coitus – published in Vienna in 1907 shortly after Freud's *Three Essays on the Theory of Sexuality* – every single position is marked with a special sign to indicate whether or not it can reasonably be conducted in a railway compartment.

Freud's phobia of trains is well known, and several different interpretations have been given over the years, but Weckerle's coding sheds new light on this. In the late nineteenth and early twentieth century, a huge amount of prostitution was carried out not just around stations but on trains – a new and unusual social space where a man and woman could be alone together – and hence the prospect of a business trip by rail almost automatically included the possibility and perhaps temptation of sexual services. When Freud got sweaty before a train ride, this may well have been the key factor, especially when we remember that he published an account of his experience of disorientation and confusion when, trying to leave the red-light district of an Italian town, he found himself returning to it inadvertently.

Western cultural scripts not only dictate places but sequences. In one popular ordering of events, each step is clearly set out: first kissing, then touching of the upper part of the body through clothes, then touching of the upper body beneath clothes, then touching the genitals through clothes, then touching of the genitals beneath clothes, then disrobing, then some form of genital penetration, and then some kind of talking. Such scripts have gender roles heavily wired into them, with males and females supposed to do different things at different moments in the sequence, together with script variations factoring in for the ages of those involved.

If a script can confer erotic value on some aspect of an encounter – or help to shape it – it can also de-eroticize. In many societies, couples help each other to undress before sex, and this process usually forms part of the erotic sequence itself. A man complained of his loss of arousal when, arriving at someone's house for a hook-up, he was instantly told at the door: 'Strip.' The action of disrobing or mutual disrobing was here quite literally stripped of its intersubjective charge, although for another person the impersonal command may well have amplified the arousal. Curiously, couples tend not to help each other get dressed again after sex – as this is not part of the script – yet we could imagine that if a 'getting dressed' scene was made erotic in some Netflix show or movie it might then enter the cultural script and acquire a sexual value.

Stephanie Theobald – author of the remarkable study of orgasm, *Sex Drive* – remembers a sketch by the comedian Ken Dodd from the 1970s in which a lustful couple progressively put on more and more clothes, panting and sighing as they add each additional layer, and then, once fully dressed, collapse exhausted on the bed. The laughs rely on the inversion of the standard script, but show how convention and sequence structure sexual relations so that a dichotomy between natural and artificial behaviour can hardly be made.

The recent TV series *Naked Attraction* uses this sequential aspect of sexual scripts as its premiss. The show is presented as 'dating in reverse', so that rather than meeting for a drink, getting to know each other, then perhaps disrobing, it begins with the disrobing and works its way up to meeting for a drink. Contestants view a series of opaque booths, each containing a naked person, with the first reveal making only their genitals visible. More body parts are revealed as the game continues, with candidates progressively eliminated, and the contestant will then choose their dream date, and off they go to meet in a public place fully clothed.

The strapline for the show is that 'We start where a good date ends', but presumably a good date doesn't end with a sequestered sighting of a person's genitals, and it is interesting to see how audiences react to the programme. The effects are described as quite the opposite of erotic, more like participation in a childhood pantomime, with giggling, screaming, gasping and cajoling, and in one case a circumcised man fainted at the sight of the 'black space' created at the aperture of the foreskin of the penises on display. 'I couldn't believe it,' he said. 'There was a hole at the end of their dicks, I couldn't look any more.'

Conventional scripts here may offer a measure of psychological safety, with genital access often carefully positioned at a late point in the sequence – and in conditions of light or darkness – but this can of course vary culturally and historically, and a script may encode a coercion to follow it through for one or both parties. Scripts both mitigate and increase risk, offering a framework for behaviour, yet exerting a pressure to follow the sequence, sometimes beyond the point at which one or both participants would rather say, 'Stop.'

*

Scripts may also include metrics of evaluation, ranging from the actual monetary pricing of women in some societies to the grading of women common in male homosocial circles. I am continually amazed to overhear educated and apparently 'woke' men here in London grade women, often with one grade for face and one for body, only to abruptly end the conversation if a woman enters the listening space, which then becomes respectful and polite. Presumably the gradings function to reinforce male group membership, through the denigration of women, while at the same time keeping the spectre of homoerotic attractions at bay, as we shall see later on. Men's sexual relations with women here seem to occur in order to talk about them with other men, and, as Margaret Mead noted long ago, securing sex membership may be more important in this context than sex itself.

If gradings among groups of men tend to occur in a confined and semi-private space, they may also be entirely public in the old 'beauty' contests and pageants that still exist in many countries. They have also been the object of some controversy in the sex industry, where reviews of sex acts with prostitutes are posted online in most countries with liberal internet access. Condemned widely as an objectifying and cruel practice – including at times contemptuous attitudes to consent – some escorts are in favour of reviews, as this not only has the potential to increase business but is also felt to be validating. Escorts in analysis often speak proudly of positive reviews, and will post replies and comments to respond to negative assessments (if the website allows this).

These reviews tend to fall into two groups. On the one hand, descriptions which are really just consolidations of the client's ego, reporting their multiple sex acts and prowess; and on the other, compliments paid to the escort, with a focus on personality, particular body parts and personal skills. Overtly negative and insulting reviews are rare. Curiously, a common feature here is an odd contextualization of events. 'It was a pleasant two-minute walk from the tube station to X's apartment'; 'The bathroom was clean with an agreeable shower gel'; 'A 7-Eleven is conveniently located about a minute away'; 'Local transport services are excellent'; 'Furniture was functional but nonetheless comfortable'. These framing devices not only reveal something of the priorities of the client but also serve to create a group, as if the idea of sharing travel tips were slightly safer than that of sharing the woman, even if that is obviously what is on the horizon of such narratives.

If we turn now to intrapsychic codes, these are established less by culture than by the circumstances of individual parenting. If one's mother or father had some physical feature or spoke in a certain way or looked at you with a specific kind of gaze, this could then become crystallized into an erotic value, something searched for in every sexual situation. The intrapsychic aspect of sexual scripting was not confined to single details or traits, but could include our need to repeat whole-sale dynamics from one's family history or even those we had heard about but never actually witnessed. Someone might create a situation in which they are always rejected, for example, or in which they always leave the partner after a one-night stand.

A woman whose love life was filled with the sorrow of broken relationships saw very clearly the pattern of her distress. She would start dating full of optimism and hope, and very quickly decide that the new partner was the right person for her. Things would go well for a while until, just at the moment when a commitment was required – such as moving in together – she would leave without understanding why. Analytic work allowed her to trace this to events that had taken place long before her own birth. Her mother had been in love with a man who had suddenly broken off their engagement, and she had then turned to the father as 'a kind of compensation, not what she wanted'. The mother's regret was often openly evoked, so that love and loss were more or less equated: the true partner was the one she no longer had, exactly the scenario that the daughter would act out in her own broken relationships.

These intrapsychic scripts determine a large part of our lives, and therapy is often crucial in helping the person to realize what they are and to untangle them. But because the intrapsychic is only one dimension of scripts, even if we succeed in gaining perspective on how some childhood beliefs and patterns have shaped us, change might be difficult or blocked entirely. Cultural codes are so pervasive and powerful that they can continue to organize our behaviour well beyond any conscious decision to disengage. And this is where the intersubjective becomes decisive.

The intersubjective dimension of a sexual script is what happens when scripts meet: people might change their behaviour, the way they were thinking and what they felt through interaction. Although there are plenty of examples of those who just stick to one single reductive script throughout their lives, many people change and experiment, and what they actually do in their sexual activity will depend on what their partner is doing, wants to do or avoid doing. We often hear about a sexual life that has been changed radically through some unexpected encounter with another person's script, and it is a question of what remains after such a reconfiguring.

A man who had always tried to impose control in his sexual life, instructing his partners what to do, was stunned when the person he was just about to script turned to him and said forcefully, 'Kiss me.' The categorical tone was hardly what he was expecting, and it marked a change in his sexual practices. He would seek out men who would repeat this same moment of reversal: 'I'd always been the active one, imposing my will, but now I want to be told what to do, I want that second when everything changes.'

The idea of sexual scripting is not meant to suggest that everything is predetermined, and Gagnon and Simon were careful to point out that scripts are never complete or comprehensive, and may change over the course of a life. Someone might shift some aspect of their sexual orientation due to a process of internal change rather than the belated expression of a 'repressed' desire. It is interesting to observe here how a woman might describe her choice of a relationship with another woman as the result of a series of disappointments from men, although we almost never find the opposite: a man won't say he chose a male partner after a series of disappointments from women.

Scripts always have lines missing, and the collision of scripts will have unpredictable results. Take the script for sexual sequences that starts with kissing and moves through to genital penetration. It doesn't tell us what to do afterwards: should we make polite conversation, clean up stains and body fluid, smoke a cigarette or vape, have a drink, share the bathroom or not, leave the bathroom door open or closed, refer to what has just happened or pretend that nothing really has? And during the sequence itself, if we have had oral contact with the other person's sex, should we kiss them directly afterwards or avoid this? If we have swallowed sperm or vaginal fluid, what is the protocol on what to do next? Should we wipe our mouth? If we've been bitten, is it OK to bite back?

This becomes even more complicated if more than two parties are involved. A male analysand was delighted when the app for threesomes first appeared in the UK, as it corresponded to his – and many other men's – phantasy. But he was swiftly both confused and unsettled when he realized that every move, every touch, every kiss, now became a choice, with the risk of making one of the two other people feel excluded. There was just no script for what the order of sexual acts should be with this multiplication of partners. Did he spend too long kissing or licking one person at the expense of the other? And this meant, of course, that he then had to spend what he considered an equal amount of time on the other person, although this was not what he wanted to be doing. During these sex acts, he continually identified with the person who was not included, and so became desperate to create parity, rather like a parent who feels guilty at favouring one child over another.

And if scripts organize our erotic life, what are the effects on sexuality when they are broken or inverted? Many men in the 1970s complained of a loss of arousal as women became more active and vocal about their desires, as the scripts for female–male interactions were changing. The convulsive laughter in porn cinemas reported at the time has been explained as an effect of an erosion of class barriers, but we could see it also as a reaction to this new articulation of desire. When the audience fell about laughing when actress Terri Hall said in a posh voice, 'I want you to lick my pussy,' it may well have been shocking to hear such language spoken by an apparently educated upper-class character, but it was surely the agency expressed that was equally, if not more, disorienting. Interestingly, over time, there was a steady decline in laughter in porn cinemas, so that watching porn became a more silent activity.

Script changes are rarely predictable in their effects here. One person may need a tight script to sustain arousal, and lose interest if it is compromised, whereas another may experience a powerful excitement at exactly the moment when the script breaks down. If one partner disrupts the expected sequence by touching the other's genitals before even kissing, this may be incredibly erotic for one person and a huge turn-off for another, in the same way that it may indeed constitute an assault. So both following a script and losing a script can have massive and at times incalculable effects.

This has important consequences for the idea of sex education. Being told what to do, what happens, what we might expect to feel and how we should treat others is essentially a script, which we are encouraged to learn and obey. But if sexuality is built up in our childhoods around precisely what isn't said, what is masked and hidden, surrounded with an atmosphere of negativity and judgement, there will always be a dimension of sex that clashes with external scripts, linked to things we have glimpsed, speech we have overheard, offhand remarks that have stayed with us.

The very fact that sex is reduced to information will render whatever is clearly said unsatisfactory and wanting, as we saw with Nora Ephron's

account of her sex education: to be told that the
penis enters the vagina was not an explanation at
all, and we could also think here of the scene in
Monty Python's *The Meaning of Life* where a
sex-ed class stare out of the window in boredom
while their teacher and his wife copulate in front
of them. The hidden, negative dimension is
what creates sexuality, and it is then a question
of how this will both shape and allow later sexual practices. Lack of confidence in one's own
body image is not the only reason why so much
sexual activity has to take place in the dark.

*

Sexual scripts can have powerful effects in culture. Take the question of orgasm. In the latter
part of the twentieth century, this became a central motif in almost all public discussions of
sexuality. If men had always taken it for granted,
what about women? Surely they had just as much
a right to orgasm as men. This could create a cultural climate in which women's sexuality was on
the agenda – a good thing – but in which there

was a new premium set on having an orgasm: if you missed out, there must be something wrong with you or your partner (usually you). The focus on orgasm thus introduced a new calculus of guilt and failure, which sex therapists noted at the time.

Orgasm itself became part of a script, popularized by Masters and Johnson with their sequence: 'arousal–plateau–climax–resolution'. They focused on orgasm in part because it could be seen and logged, identifying it with involuntary muscular contractions despite the fact that it was well known that women could experience orgasm without these behavioural signs. It was also well documented that, for males, ejaculation and orgasm were not one continuous physiological process and that the one could occur without the other. Yet Masters and Johnson opted for streamlining, and sex now meant moving through these scripted physiological thresholds in a linear way.

Sex, as Gagnon and Simon pointed out, was here given an Aristotelian structure, like some kind of stage play or drama, though without the category of an obstacle that drama theorists had found necessary for plots to work. And, like a stage play, emotions and states of arousal could – and perhaps even needed to be – faked. Where faking virginity had for centuries been a serious task, with high stakes, the emphasis now was on faking orgasm, and the more pressure there was to conform to the orgasm narrative, the more that women – and occasionally men – felt obliged to fake it. This became such an ingrained part of sexual practice that when the French writer Marie Darrieussecq published a story about a woman who fakes *not* having orgasms, the reaction was utter disbelief.

Once sex had this new dramatic structure, one could of course fail at each point in the sequence, and problems in sex were swiftly identified with performance anxieties. We could think here of the little *mamesuke* figures in Japanese erotic art, who crowd round the lovers offering comments like 'He's not doing too well, is he?' or 'A bit late for that now, eh!' Peering from under mats and from over screens, they materialize humorously the idea that sex is a performance or demonstration that we feel is constantly being watched and evaluated.

If as a society we had turned our most intimate moments into tests or demonstrations, the new imperative of the late 1960s and 70s was to have sex without trying to perform or prove anything. As psychoanalyst Bernard Apfelbaum observed, people used to feel ashamed at not being able to perform, yet now they were also ashamed of wanting to perform. This, of course, was a much taller order than proving, say, virility, since proving that you are not proving anything is more or less impossible. Sex without a script to perform was thus even more of a script, with an even greater toll on the players, as some of the more astute sex therapists noticed. To say that sex was really all about intimacy was just giving the criterion by which the test was to be graded, and as Apfelbaum added, why tell the patient in sex therapy that they are afraid of intimacy, as if they shouldn't be!

The emphasis on performance and evaluation perhaps explains the quite extraordinary change in the statistics for the length of penetrative sex in the early 1970s. Where Kinsey had found some twenty-five years previously that the average duration of penis-in-vagina coitus was just less than two minutes, when Morton and Bernice Hunt conducted their survey of American sexual practices in 1973, the figure had become twelve minutes, not including foreplay! Looking at the data, it was in fact the men who said twelve while the women put it at fifteen, suggesting that they might have experienced it as longer, or too long. Whatever the case, recent figures set the clock back to around five minutes, so either we need to hypothesize a bizarre and temporary socio-biological change in the human species in the early 1970s or, more likely, see in the inflated figures a reflection of the new emphasis on performing and evaluating.

We could think here of the old story of the sex-education lecture in a New England ladies' college. After detailing the dangers of premarital sex and the catastrophic consequences that could ensue, the principal concludes her talk with the warning, 'So think carefully, think twice, when a man bothers you – is all this really worth it for an hour of pleasure?' When she invites questions, a voice from the back of the hall asks: 'How do you make it last an hour?'

*

The fact that the time required for men and women to reach orgasm was quite different further complicated any idea of a simultaneous explosion of pleasure. The early generations of psychoanalysts hadn't helped too much here, with their canonical separation of clitoral and vaginal orgasms, although some writers like Marjorie Brierley had disagreed, emphasizing rather the coordination between the vagina and the clitoris. According to the popular dogma, a woman must learn to move from the immature and boyish clitoral sexuality of childhood to the new vaginal sexuality of adulthood, shifting her bodily innervations from the one to the other. Freud claimed that the sexual life of many women was 'crippled' by their clinging to clitoral arousal, and that vaginal receptivity signalled a passage to femininity. Writing before the wider public recognition and marketing of female orgasm, he spoke about a primacy of erotogenic zones – so preferences – rather than orgasm as such.

Some analysts, on the contrary, argued that vaginal sensitivity was absolutely present in early childhood, and that both forms of excitation retained their importance throughout life. Everyone was apparently disproved here when Masters and Johnson claimed in the mid 1960s that clitoral and vaginal were basically the same thing anatomically, with clitoral stimulation the source of both kinds of orgasm. Piston-like movement of the penis would impact soft perineal tissue adjacent to the clitoral hood, and hence – indirectly – the glans clitoris itself. The Danish sex educators Inge and Sten Hegeler had argued the same point in their *ABZ of Love* some years earlier, yet their message had to wait for the glossier American research with its scientific wrapping and lab-coated authors. At the same time, the psychiatrist Mary Jane Sherfey – famous for defining vibrator use as 'nymphomania without promiscuity' – stressed the biological unity of the clitoris and the lower third of the vagina, and Shere Hite explained in her widely read *Report* in 1976 that vaginal penetration just spread the sensations from direct or indirect clitoral arousal.

Later studies would show that the clitoris was much more than an isolated 'pleasure button', with substantial roots and legs extending along and within the labia and parts of the vaginal wall. Rather than a pea – like in the story of what the princess can feel under all those mattresses – it was now compared to a person with long slinky arms, like the wall-crawler that delights children, or to an octopus. With more research and imaging of the anatomy and innervation of the clitoris, it was argued that the so-called vaginal orgasm is simply a product of the impact of the clitoral root on the anterior vaginal wall. Case closed.

The cultural script here has direct effects on sexual life, as people learn to evaluate their feelings and actions in terms of what scientific authorities tell them about the body. But the facts here are both helpful and unhelpful. Those who have suffered spinal injuries which effectively block any nervous transmission from the genitals can still report experiencing orgasm, and there is in general a two- to four-second gap between the feeling of orgasm and the actual physiological changes that Masters and Johnson recorded. Breastfeeding women, likewise, occasionally report an orgasm, despite the absence of any genital stimulation, as do women withdrawing from morphine.

Similarly, an orgasm, together with all the signs of physical exertion and cardiorespiratory escalation, can occur in the absence of any body movement: just visual attention to an arousing film, for example. Women here can orgasm watching porn or entertaining a phantasy, with no genital stimulation, something that men are usually unable to do (with some celebrated exceptions, like Jean Cocteau and Samuel Johnson). Sex activist and performance artist Carol Queen describes how, with the right sexual energy from a client, she could orgasm simply by stroking her foot when doing peep-show work. Whatever the cultural script dictates – and today it often has the biological veneer of Masters and Johnson's approach – women's actual experience of orgasm is in many cases different. Rather than telling them that they must be mistaken, which is what some experts are prone to do, it is surely worth listening to what they are saying.

With orgasm, women tend to distinguish different kinds of experience. The popular vaginal–clitoral binary provides a framework here, but one which is both contradictory and reductive, as there are innumerable permutations, and it is quite striking to see how the vocabulary used for the one may be the same as the vocabulary used for the other. Clitoral orgasm can be described as 'more intense', 'sharp', 'dramatic', 'electrical' or 'hot', with vaginal 'less intense', 'deep', 'throbbing' or 'soothing', but the very same terms can be applied by other women to the apparently opposite experiences. Vaginally-induced orgasms could be described as 'stronger' by 40 per cent of women in one study and 'weaker' by 42 per cent. Herschberger had warned years before this research that binaries were not an appropriate framework for studying female sexuality, and Selma Fraiberg had noted the 'astonishingly rich vocabulary' of young girls to differentiate feelings associated with vaginal exploration from other kinds of 'good feeling'.

While female orgasm is often equated culturally with some kind of ecstatic experience, it may
also be felt as deadening or unwanted, even distant from the body, which may be described as
'foreign', 'strange' or 'dead'. For those studying
this in terms of the vaginal–clitoral binary, vaginal orgasm has been said to correlate more closely
with a worldview where excitement, tension and
arousal are minimal, which is taken to then refute
the old psychoanalytic dogma that 'vaginal'
women are more mature or better adjusted than
the clitorally-oriented. Most of this research is
quite dubious, but it aimed at least to challenge
the segregation of women into classes evaluated
by male judges.

Orgasm, indeed, is almost always deemed
secondary by women in sexual-satisfaction surveys, and only one in five rate orgasm as the most
important source of sexual pleasure. In sex with
men, orgasm may only occur about 25 per cent of
the time at best. The male training to see penile
ejaculation as both the apex and the end point of
sexual contact tends to entail a lack of sensitivity
to the multilocal nature of female arousal, and to

non-genital sources of pleasure. Where men often have a hydraulic conception of sexuality, with orgasm relieving tension, they are less alert to the dimension of meaning, and the effects that this can have on female arousal. Trust, after all, is a meaning, and one which can be the key factor in enabling sexual pleasure in some cases.

Arguing against Masters and Johnson, Josephine and Irving Singer observed this importance of the emotional dimension, where the meaning of sex acts cannot be disassociated from their physiology. Questioning simplistic and arbitrary definitions of female orgasm, they emphasized the multiplicity of its forms, and the mistaken equation with involuntary perineal or vaginal contractions: an orgasm is no less 'real' in the absence of muscular convulsions. These may occur without any sense of pleasure, yet laboratory studies of sex were unable to factor in the question of satisfaction here as they had no way to assess the role of emotion.

Hoping to go beyond the vaginal–clitoral binary, the Singers distinguished three kinds of orgasm: vulval – manifested in muscular contractions after clitoral stimulation; uterine – characterized by emotional reactions, and gasping followed by breath-holding, with no contractions; and blended – a mixture of both previous forms, with contractions and apnoea accompanied by a sense of 'heaving', deeper than a vulval orgasm. As one woman put it, 'My vagina swallows one or two times and I have an orgasm.'

The changes in breathing that characterize the uterine and blended forms involve what the Singers term 'laryngeal displacement', brief repetitive apnoeas where each gasp adds to the amount of breath held in the lungs, drawing the larynx down and back to produce a feeling of 'strangling in ecstasy'. Then the cricopharyngeus – the upper oesophageal sphincter – snaps back to a resting position and the breath is exhaled explosively, a sequence very different from the typical panting kind of hyperventilation of the vulval orgasm. Just as Theophrastus had once suggested classifying flowers by their smell rather than the shape and colour of their petals, the Singers' work invites us to classify orgasms less by the genital

area stimulated than by the differential patterns
of breathing, and their emotional resonance.

What they term laryngeal displacement,
indeed, occurs also in grief, surprise, fear and joy,
and hence the way that some women may describe
orgasm as 'nothing but emotion'. In Doris Lessing's words, 'A vaginal orgasm is emotion and
nothing else, felt as emotion and expressed in sensations that are indistinguishable from emotion.'
Tears and sobbing may follow, and Lessing notes
how the facial expression with this kind of orgasm
is one of fear, with the corners of the lips drawn
back, while with a clitoral orgasm the teeth are
bared and the brow furrowed, as if in anger.

Men are often perplexed at the curious admix-
ture of tears, grief and joy that can accompany
female orgasm, reactions that hardly ever follow
male ejaculation and that may indeed remove a
man's erection. When we explore a bit further,
we often find that the tears index a deep sense
of potential loss: not loss of the man's actual
penis but of his presence, his life, his love. The
experience of such powerful and unparalleled
intimacy – which can occur just as or even more

frequently in female–female sexual relationships – quite literally brings with it the spectre of
its loss, and hence, perhaps, the temporary
feeling of grief. But this grief can be inflected
by other, equally complex emotions.

A woman in therapy with Edrita Fried
explained how at times her partner felt 'too
close' – to make her wonder 'Who am I? Where
am I?' – and would take refuge in brief relations
with male lovers, precisely to save herself from
the terrifying feeling of losing herself in intimacy: 'They frighten me less because there is no
closeness.' When she was too close, 'There is no
me.' This question of boundaries was beautifully
described by a patient of Edith Jacobson who differentiated closeness, likeness, sameness and
oneness: 'Close is close, as with you; when you
are like somebody, you are only *like* the other,
you and he are two; sameness – you are the same
as the other, but he is still he and you are you; but
oneness is not two – it is one, it is one, that's
horrible – horrible!' she exclaimed as she leapt up
from the couch in a sudden panic.

If a merging of boundaries can be terrifying,

Darian Leader

hostility to the sexual partner may form part of the sexual experience, and we find again and again both this feeling of reproach and another, perhaps different form of hatred. An analysand would masturbate with no phantasy except an intense feeling of hate towards her mother, 'as if I was hating her with my clitoris'. This is rare but other analysts have noticed how hate can fuse with excitement, and Anaïs Nin famously wrote in *Delta of Venus* that 'the orgasm had been so strong that she thought she would go insane, with a hatred and joy like nothing she had ever known'. Is this the hatred generated by the loss of boundaries or something else?

*

The question of faking orgasm opens up the broader question of truth and authenticity. As the sex therapists of the 1970s were aware, the new imperatives of the authenticity movement to 'be real' and 'true to oneself' simply tied people in knots. One could become even more self-conscious in sex by trying to get rid of all self-consciousness.

Sexual role plays had a special appeal here as they short-circuited this problem: all parties were acting, so sex lost the mandate to be genuine. Many people still find that role playing is the optimal way to relate sexually to others, as self-consciousness, embarrassment and performing are no longer anomalies but part of the script itself.

But even in a role play, orgasm is supposed to be genuine, so the question of truth is not entirely removed. When adults act out doctor–patient, teacher–student or boss–employee scenarios, the micro-dramas that they stage tend to culminate in orgasm that is apparently genuine: the artificial framework guarantees the arousal for the non-artificial excitation. It is interesting to note that nearly all role plays involve acting out scenes that would lead to professional complaints, disgrace or imprisonment in reality, as boundaries are being transgressed and power relations exploited.

Such role plays are extraordinarily wide-spread, and may be directly proportional to the increasing seriousness with which professional boundaries – and hence taboos – are treated in society. The double standards here may not be simple hypocrisy but part of the very structure of the social world, which acts to refract desire. Compare, for example, the horrified reactions to cases of paedophilia and the violence directed to perpetrators with the fact that the best-selling product of most Western sex shops – apart from print and visual media and vibrators – has been the schoolgirl uniform.

And this brings us to the key question. How can the authenticity of orgasm be proved? How can we know for sure what is being felt and not simply shammed? A man who grew up in the bubble of his mother's unconditional love would pay prostitutes to engage in various practices which would all end in their gagging. He explained the logic of this surface sadism: everything he did was always praised by his mother and he could literally do no wrong, which made his whole life seem unreal. 'Nothing was true, it was all a fake.' Making a woman gag, however, could not be faked: it was the only proof he had of something real, something genuine that he had caused himself, a point of truth in a woman that he had been unable to find in his mother.

The pain inflicted on the woman here could certainly be described as sadistic, although the conscious aim was not to generate suffering but truth. There are other cases where the anxiety and suffering of the sexual partner are actually the desired result, and de Sade believed that since a woman's sensation of enjoyment could be faked and pain could not, pain was therefore the highest form of sexual activity. 'Fabricating', indeed, was once a term used to refer to the act of coitus itself. There is a difference here which is important clinically: the pursuit of the gagging reflex was about finding a point of authenticity, of reality, whereas the cases where the aim is to produce suffering involve an actual pleasure in the harm caused, an arousal linked to pain. In these cases, we often find a childhood history of violence, in which the person has been tortured or victimized by parents or siblings rather than unconditionally loved.

If love has been absent or entirely conditional, it may be difficult, even impossible, for the child to feel that they have been able to affect their parent, and so the only available option may seem to be the infliction of pain or, in some cases, driving them to breaking point. It is only then that they may feel that they actually exist, in that single fleeting moment of fury or despair in the other person. A man who had enjoyed strangling German soldiers with a wire in the Warsaw Ghetto would find, many years later, that his sexual excitement would crystallize into a particular scenario. He would drive round till he found an old-fashioned barber shop, and would request a wet shave. Once completed, he would say that it wasn't smooth enough and that it had to be repeated. As this process continued, he would ejaculate under the barber's sheet at the moment when it seemed as if the barber couldn't take it any more and would himself lose control. He'd pay and return home.

The excitement here was linked both to the risk of death – he'd imagine that the barber might be so exasperated that he'd cut his throat with the razor – and to the imposition of his own command, overriding the barber's subjectivity to a point that would be unbearable. His own control and his fear of the other's loss of control converged at the same place, the moment that guaranteed his orgasm, and we might wonder what this tells us about orgasm itself: should we see it as an experience of pleasure and satisfaction or as a treatment of anxiety and terror, or conclude, perhaps, that there is actually no difference here between the two?

The role of pain in sexual life cannot be predicted from childhood history. There is no rule that dictates whether a person who has had great pain inflicted on them will later choose to inflict pain on others or seek to have pain inflicted again upon themselves. The vicissitudes of each person's history will inform such a choice, and there may equally be an avoidance of pain altogether. Scripts can change, and rarely pass unadulterated from one generation to the next, just as commitments – like that to gagging – can appear as a result of random events and only later come to embody a key condition of arousal.

But sexual scenarios do have a special place here, as they represent privileged moments of intimacy. What this means is that they become particularly suited to play out dramas of acceptance and rejection, of being chosen and then dropped. If someone is deprived of the power in their everyday life of, say, humiliating others, sex may end up being the only space where this becomes momentarily possible. A power relation can be established and enjoyed however briefly, where the person probably occupies both places at once: the one being humiliated and dropped and the one doing the humiliating and dropping.

The clue here to the duality of places can be clear in the emotion afterwards: guilt and, often, laughter. In Milgram's notorious experiments in which male subjects were asked to administer electric shocks to their peers, pressing switches with labels like 'Intense Shock' and 'Danger: Severe Shock', he noticed in those – the majority – who increased the voltage that they would laugh sometimes uncontrollably while they were doing it: 'the laughter seemed entirely out of place, even bizarre'. This was presumably a sign of identification with their victims, as if they were in both places at once. Gershon Legman, commenting on this, pointed out the apparent absence of laughter in concentration-camp personnel charged with pumping Zyklon B into the gas chambers. They were not divided by laughter as they were not divided by identification with their victims, and hence, perhaps, how they were able to do their job so effortlessly.

*

Let's see how this dynamic of scripts and commitments might operate for boys. In patriarchal societies, most accounts tell us that boys have been traditionally socialized right from the start to value aggression and dominance. The penis is a weapon to be used in their service, and sex is understood as an act of possession. Little attention is accorded to female pleasure, and the woman's body is seen as a vessel for male enjoyment and nothing more. In this version of male sexuality, the distance between coitus and rape is quite slim.

Now, there is little doubt that this conception of male sexuality and the power differential it is based on has been and still is widespread. It has been estimated that for each joke in which the penis has some capacity to please a woman, there are ten in which it is used to harm, impale or kill her. Yet what anthropologists, historians and analysts have found is that beneath the surface a lot more is going on. Along with cultural and temporal variation, surface behaviour doesn't always reveal what is at stake, and perhaps the first point to be made is that all human sexual orientations are not based on innate copulatory instincts but on fear.

This was nicely brought out in a seven-year-old child's description of their own position: 'I'm really interested in sexuality. I'm non-binary myself, but you can be trans, queer, lesbian, hetero, bisexual or homophobic.' Homophobia was understood as an orientation in itself, as if fear and bias could be a defining feature of sexual identity. Sexual scripts can encode and transmit such fears, aiming to create and maintain boundaries and offering a compass for us, a guide through the terrifying landscape of changes in our own bodies and the interaction with other people's. For boys, there is the well-known fear of bodily damage – famously identified with castration by

Freud — but also the more archaic terror of genital, anal and abdominal penetration.

Two- to three-year-olds are especially vocal in their concerns about breaches to the body boundary, with aggressors usually identified with animals or bad people who bite and devour. Most stories children devise around this age involve hurt or mutilation, and researchers have noted the glee in atrocities, as boys marshal weapons that pierce and penetrate. By five, the threats have become more abstract, such as an earthquake, floods, fires, tsunami or nuclear war, and dangerous characters in their stories become less identifiable. Boys describe misfortunes much more often than girls, although girls seem more interested than boys in remedying or curing the bad stuff that happens, and in understanding exactly how it occurred.

Loss of body parts is a much more common theme for boys than it is for girls, and by adolescence, jokes and 'true stories' tend to centre around genital injuries, anal penetration, horrific accidents and bodily mutilations. The rapid way in which these are passed around and circulated testifies to the pressure to spread the anxiety and guilt evoked by sexual thoughts as widely as possible. And at the same time, it creates fragile membership systems, through affirming shared anxieties and through the exclusion and denigration of girls and women.

Researching this book, I was surprised to find that practically all the studies of bodily boundaries, from the 1950s until today, suggested that male boundaries were experienced as much more porous than female. This seemed to clash not only with psychoanalytic work, which emphasized the anxiety around vaginal penetration, but also with the apparent attention to the body surface displayed by many women, reinforced by the cosmetics industry, and also with the long history of rites and customs to maintain female body boundaries, as seen in the old insistence on virginity at marriage.

This often meant, however, a purely perceived virginity, as a very high number of church marriages – between 20 per cent and 50 per cent in the early modern period – occurred when the bride was already pregnant, and some social groups even opted to select only one woman to retain bodily virginity, making her a symbol, and thus removing the sanctions on others for premarital sex. The focus on 'public' virginity here can be seen as a reflection of male social imperatives, and it was only very recently that rape has come to be considered a crime against women rather than a crime against the man who owned the woman. Loss of virginity meant a loss of or reduction in the socio-economic value of the bride in many cultures, and punishments ranged from execution of the culprit to severe financial penalty.

Curiously, although we seem to have moved beyond this in our enlightened times, the investment in virginal purity is pervasive: at weddings, the bridal veil is clearly a symbol of the hymenal membrane, and the plate smashing and glass breaking that form part of the wedding party in many cultures represent breaking of the seal of virginity. Similarly, as Gershon Legman pointed out, the gesture of carrying the bride across the threshold in fact means crossing the threshold of the bride. Even in the supermarket, many products have a notice that instructs customers to return the product should they find that the seal is broken, surely a relic of the cult of hymenal intactness.

Yet the porosity of the male body should not be underestimated, and we could think here of the many cultural images of a body inside a body, from *Avatar* to *Pacific Rim*, in which one male body is housed inside another robotic one. Enhancing the man's power, the exoskeleton also provides a rigid bodily envelope, creating a solid boundary at the point of possible invasion. Even the old-school insignia of male power – the phallus – can be a conduit to these vulnerabilities, as we see in the common dream motif of the penis being open and penetrable through the urethra. Like the doubling of the body itself, there are also often childhood phantasies of a penis encased within a penis.

The fear of invasion here can be linked to both external and internal forces. A young patient of Selma Fraiberg understood perfectly that pregnancy involved sperm and fertilization, yet assumed that sperm is contained within the penis itself. Just as the mother's body would be cut open to let the baby out, he explained, so too the penis would have to be cut open to release the sperm, which he imagined as being the size of a marble. This magnification was based on a book about reproduction which his mother had read him, and which had clearly stated that the marble-sized image was taken with a microscope, sperm themselves being too tiny to actually see. His anxieties about the body had shaped what information he could absorb, and his terror of damage to the penis was hardly mitigated.

It is perhaps the effort to maintain these fragile bodily boundaries that so often results in violence. Boys have dreadful fears of damage to a part of the body, and of bursting open and losing their viscera. They fear invasion by a male penis, and one could even argue that male sexuality is a complex structure the main purpose of which is to defend against these early terrors. The fears themselves may derive from parental handling of the child's body and attitudes towards it, fear of retaliation for rage against the parent, or archaic forms of identification with the mother, who is herself assumed to be open to penetration. When the protagonist in the film *Ted* explains to his talking teddy bear that he's planning something really really special for his girlfriend, the teddy assumes that this means anal penetration, as if this lay at the horizon of all other sexual acts.

We should remember here that both boys and girls start out so close to the mother that identifications with her must be inevitable: whereas the girl might not feel pressured to change her sex here, boys are socialized to separate, to dis-identify from her, often using cultural ideas of masculine behaviour. As Margaret Mead noted, this has often been interpreted too hastily as an effort to identify with the father and to take his place, whereas it may also be a more basic way of finding a counterpoint to the mother's 'maternity': there is thus a difference between wanting *to be* someone and wanting *not to be* someone, which can impact how a child inhabits the gender roles that they assume.

Masculinity is an artificial construction here, a defence, and therefore inherently fragile, and the efforts to stay masculine may even involve a re-inforcement of peril. If the child is worried about some sort of violent reprisal from the father or bodily damage due to their claims on the mother, they may offer themselves up as a sexual object: 'I'm not a threat, just love me!' But this of course carries the new risk of being penetrated, and so the very manoeuvre designed to keep the boy safe leaves him effectively open to attack.

Sexual humour is an invaluable source of insight here into unconscious aspects of sexuality, and the following joke brings out the male dynamic very clearly. 'An actor must lose forty pounds fast to play Hamlet. At a luxurious gym he is offered a twelve-hour crash course for $1,000 or a twenty-four-hour course for $500. He chooses the twenty-four-hour course and is ushered naked into a large empty room with a padded table at the centre. The door opens and a beautiful naked woman enters wearing only a sign over her breasts: "You catch me, you fuck me." Wondering what he must have missed in refusing to pay the extra $500, he tells her to go back and send him the director, to whom he explains that he has reconsidered and would prefer the $1,000 option. He is taken to another, identical room and locked in. A door opens at the far end and a gigantic ape with an enormous erection enters, wearing only a sign: "I catch you, I fuck you."'

Once again, the joke suggests that at the horizon of a man's sexual desire for a woman is the terror of being anally penetrated by another man, so that the very idea that a woman might seek vaginal penetration may well be a male phantasy: the man's fear of being anally penetrated is projected on to the women, with the fear changed into 'desire'. It is she who wants penetration, not him. Thus, the ubiquitous male idea that women want to be penetrated, even when they are saying No, may be an ascription of their own fear–desire outside themselves: by making women 'want' penetration, they worry less about being penetrated themselves. This is called 'defensive masculinity', although it should be obvious by now that the expression is a pleonasm: masculinity is in itself a defence.

This would explain why machismo posturing always seems so theatrical and absurd, as if there is nothing natural about it and the artificial dimension is at such high density. Those men who find themselves at the apex of socially invested power – primarily Premier League footballers and High Court judges – pay female sex workers to anally penetrate them with a strap-on with an extraordinary frequency. It is as if the theatrical dimension of masculinity here coalesces with a certain image of femaleness – or simply with an inversion of power – and the phallus is revealed as an artificial prop. Interestingly, although this was once the service of choice for male Westminster politicians in the UK, there has apparently been a decline over the last twenty years, a reflection most probably of the steady erosion of their personal power due to transparency protocols and sustained media and web-based scrutiny.

Anal penetration is also surely one of the reasons for the bizarre popularity of the film *Pulp Fiction*. All the funny chit-chat and quaint situations that fans make so much of merely form a kind of diversion from the central scene in which the powerful macho gangster played by Ving Rhames is anally raped. When Bruce Willis's character picks up a sword to rescue him, the audience excitement at the prospect of a violent revenge using a weapon perhaps represents the other side of the act of rape that has just taken place: to pierce rather than to be pierced.

On this model, male heterosexual desire is more about keeping other men at the right distance than any real interest in a woman, although of course this can change over time. When male teenagers have sex, the first thing they do is tell their friends, as if the value of the act lies more in relating to the male friendship group and positioning oneself there than in any bodily or intersubjective pleasure. The really shocking thing about the first sex scene between Marianne and Connell in the TV adaptation of Sally Rooney's *Normal People* was the fact that it cut immediately afterwards to a shot of him and his friends bantering and he said nothing about what had just happened.

This framing can happen before, during and after a sex act, as the phenomenon of sex tapes shows so clearly. In the well-known Ray J–Kim Kardashian tape, he prefaces the video with a greeting to all the guys who are going to be jerking off to it later on, as if this is the actual reason for staging the event. Sex with a woman is what reinforces membership of the male group, while simultaneously treating the dangers of homoerotic proximity. We could remember here that blue movies objectifying women were traditionally shown to groups of men rather than to individuals, in the US at business and political conventions, and in the UK more frequently at parties.

Male group membership is consolidated not only by sex with women – and sharing images of this – but also by acts of manifest destruction. We are all horrified by the treatment of so-called witches in the past, and recognize that they were often women who challenged in some way the norms and values of patriarchy. But burning a witch still remains part of family entertainment today. In the most recent addition to the *Ghostbusters* franchise – *Afterlife* – the film concludes with a scene in which the three surviving male ghostbusters fry a female demon with massive electrical charges. As she writhes in agony, the men surround her, each one shooting out a white flame of electricity from their weapons, in a symbolism that would embarrass even the most unreconstructed Freudian. The task of destroying a woman was essentially what brought the ghostbusters back together again, a male group now re-established through this act of violence. When I saw it, the audience cheered and clapped during this scene.

Note here how the current promotion of superhero-types as outsiders often conceals this hidden cruelty. Recent movies and TV series portray characters with special powers, misunderstood and persecuted by their peers. If they're lucky, they find recognition and companionship with other outcasts like themselves, as in the *X-Men* franchise or *The Umbrella Academy*, and even the old stalwarts like Batman and Superman are depicted as perpetually hounded and scapegoated. But these figures are almost always those who take the law into their own hands, and, as Sterling North pointed out way back in 1940, let's not forget that they also wear masks, making them the new representatives of the 'hooded justice' that was once the symbol of such a terrible part of American history. Although much has been made of the Jewish backgrounds of some superhero creators, these figures still occupy a similar social space in American culture: masked individuals who dispense justice beyond the law.

*

Male peer groups here are notorious for their stunted morality, and their xenophobic and cruel positioning of gay and ethnically diverse people. These constitute images of difference – and desire – which in part means sameness, the aspect of themselves that they must keep at bay and avoid thinking about, due to the terror of homosexuality contaminating heterosexuality. The male rituals at adolescence in many cultures that mark or cut the body may aim to consolidate this, assigning the boy to a male lineage, and disidentifying him from the mother.

Elements associated with femaleness may be literally beaten out of the body, and supposedly contaminating substances acquired via contact with the mother forced out of the body through vomiting, nose bleeding and skin perforation. As Ford and Beach observed in the 1940s, cishet men are socialized not to recognize homoerotic feelings within themselves to the point at which they may actually be totally unable to do so. They might feel uneasy peeing next to another man at a urinal, or get an erection watching a sporting event, but these moments are ignored and swiftly forgotten. The use of women here may be almost entirely defensive, as they are reduced to objects, a currency of the group's conversation and metric of achievements, with sex acts scored like sporting events or homicides, as men refer to 'first base', 'smashing', 'shooting' or 'body count'.

The occasional violence in male prostitution has often revolved around the same dynamic. In 'hustler'-style sex work, a young man, often homeless and impoverished, will be fellated for a fee by an older man. After payment and the conclusion of the act, the contract is terminated. But if there has been any intimation that the young man enjoyed it, or may be gay himself, violence towards the client could at times be triggered, as it may be so important to maintain the hetero–homo boundary that the comment had troubled. Hetero–homo borders are never stable, and for a man to try to maintain them rigidly will require a significant amount of energy and, at times, violence, as violence tends to be how people deal with the question of borders.

Male bar-room brawls are an obvious example of this, with the irony that the very gestures used to defend borders simultaneously violate them, as they involve physical contact with other men. When young men beat up other young men after a night out in the pub – sometimes, though by no means always, choosing gay victims – this is without any doubt an example of sexually motivated assault, even if the sexual dimension is not transparent to the aggressors. Acts such as punching, stabbing and shooting may take the place of the rejected homoerotic sex contacts. Although historically, sexual 'minorities' have so often been persecuted and identified with toxicity and danger, it is surely heterosexuality that is the real danger here, as it is the only sexual category that requires violence to determine its own boundaries.

Interestingly, we often find that sexual practices which are labelled 'gay' involve exactly this
porosity at the very point where 'het' practices aim
to negate it. If a man may be incredibly disturbed
if images of another man's penis enter his mind
while having sex with a woman, it is not uncommon, as Stephanie Theobald notes, to find a gay
woman imagining being penetrated by a man while
having sex with a woman. There may be little
incentive to broadcast these fleeting or sustained
thoughts, as they may be felt to clash with one's
gender positioning and the script that goes with it.

Although today there is more latitude, perhaps, in these scripts, the 'sex wars' of the women's
movement around female–female relations are
instructive here. It was a widely held belief that to
challenge patriarchy in any serious way meant
changing how one did sex and with whom. This
did not just mean, as Shere Hite advocated, 'less
thrusting', but the injunction, felt by many women,
to give up men altogether and enter gay relationships. All well and good, except that women who
were already in female–female relationships of
their own making often felt their sexuality was

being castigated and judged: there was a right and a wrong way to do lesbianism, and the 'new' gay women were now busy telling everyone else what the rules were.

As Gayle Rubin put it, 'By conflating lesbianism – which I think of as a sexual and erotic experience – with feminism – a political philosophy – the ability to justify lesbianism on grounds other than feminism dropped out of the discourse.' Lust itself could not be seen as a legitimating factor. What is so interesting for us here is the dichotomy between the old-school queer women – whose choice was often storied (by them) as based on Eros and passion, and (by their critics) on internalized patriarchal norms – and the new 'political lesbians' whose sexual orientation was apparently based on what was right rather than on any burning desire: so, on what Rubin calls political philosophy.

Crucially, on this reading, the new lesbians' choice was *a way of saying something*: a resounding No to patriarchy and to heterosexist relations. This was in turn deemed inauthentic by detractors and ridiculed as the false revolt of (mostly) middle-class white women, but doesn't it suggest that if adopting gay sexuality can be a way of saying something, so perhaps the same goes for straight heterosexuality. Choosing heterosexuality in childhood or adolescence could also surely be seen as a way of making a statement, of adopting unknowingly a 'political philosophy' – for one's parents, for one's peers, for one's safety – without much underlying passion, and so the new female homosexuality and the heterosexism that was being fought against perhaps shared a similar underlying structure.

The split itself between hetero and homo is in many senses a historical construction, as historians have shown how both the notions of heterosexuality and homosexuality are relatively recent ideas, in terms of a sexual identity. Engaging in same-sex acts that we might qualify as homosexual today has clearly had a very different meaning in periods of the past, although historians of sexuality disagree with how the relation between sexual acts and sexual identities has been construed. For men to practise anal intercourse, for example, in the sixteenth century might be deemed sinful in terms of a social and legal code, but it did not mean that the person was 'homosexual', as this category just didn't exist, and it might have been seen as a form of lust to which anyone might be drawn. Today it is easy to associate social identities with sexual preferences, but such equations were arguably much rarer in the past, although the Greek *kinaidos* or Roman *cinaedus* have been claimed as counter-examples, indexing a kind of male person who hires out their body for male use (yet also applied to those who pay to be penetrated anally).

To take a well-known example, Voltaire is said to have had sex with an Englishman, who asked him whether he'd like to repeat the experience. 'Doing it once, I'm a philosopher,' he allegedly replied, 'but doing it twice would make me a sodomite.' Now, should we read 'sodomite' as designating a social identity – a 'kind of person' with set ways, behaviours and social insignia – or the author of certain acts, assuming that there is a distinction between acts and identity? Yet even asking this question assumes that the distinction itself is somehow ahistorical, complicated further by the fact that the term 'sodomy' could refer to a variety of practices, including masturbation.

Curiously, making a distinction between identity and acts is arguably a characteristic feature of male sexuality: 'It was just sex', 'That's not who I am', 'I've said sorry so can we wipe the slate clean.' Sexuality is distilled to acts which the person then distances themself from, as if they have no further consequences. We see this every day in relationships, as well as in the way that men try to exonerate themselves in the media after being tarnished in some scandal. Men are constantly busy splitting, and this perhaps explains why the differentiation between acts and identity has been so popular with male academics.

We can note how this is also a significant feature of child-rearing. When a parent admonishes a child for some misdemeanour, it may be extremely difficult – and even impossible – to convince them that doing something wrong does not make them a bad person. As the parent tries to persuade them that there is a difference between acts and identity, the child may be unable to think in that way: doing something wrong means that the parent has withdrawn their love, and therefore the child is unworthy and intrinsically bad. Acts and identity here are continuous rather than disjunct. Religious cultures, with their conditional and unconditional notions of sin and guilt, only reinforce these categorical judgements.

Also crucial here is the way that we situate our binaries: do we buy into the idea of homosexuality and heterosexuality as polarities, or, like Kinsey, as somehow continuous? Readers today may be puzzled when reading fiction from the 1960s on to find a character introducing themselves with 'Hi, I'm a Kinsey Six', yet the numerical rating was so well known that it was used in personal profiles and greetings, and, of course, in jokes and gags. Seeing homosexuality and heterosexuality as a continuum, Kinsey had made a scale from 0 to 6 to indicate where one lay on the spectrum, with an additional X if sexual behaviour was avoided. Jocular use of this metric meant that one could designate oneself or others with both negative numbers and extremely large ones, just as the Xs could be multiplied.

Adopting a continuum or a polarized approach here will shape how we approach the problem of sexual identities historically, yet the very use of the binary terms themselves works implicitly to maintain the categories. Historians of sexuality have shown very clearly that using the nineteenth- and twentieth-century categories of 'hetero' and 'homo' to describe and explain other cultures and times is problematic. Sexual relations between convent nuns or medieval monks or female troubadours or Templar knights or early modern female vineyard workers or young eighteenth-century aristocrats or Castro clones cannot be explored using the same terms. If we do, we risk objectifying the categories themselves, to suggest some immutable biological or social essence, although there are plenty of people who do not see any problem with this. To say, for example, 'the cause of heterosexuality or homosexuality is X' perpetuates the idea that these are fixed underlying entities that just require explanation, rather than constructs which enforce social values.

These are not just abstract questions for historians, but will have a real and very tangible impact on all aspects of human relationships. How sexual acts acquire meaning and how this meaning is used to define identity can shape both what we feel allowed to do and what we feel allowed to feel. If the hustler did not have a modern idea of what 'homosexuality' is, he may not have reacted against it in the same way. If fellating other males, for example, were seen as an everyday part of male life with no implications for sexual relations with women, would it risk generating comparable violence?

This has in fact been a common practice in several societies, such as the Keraki and Kiwai of New Guinea, where male–male oral and anal penetration formed part of the cultural script for adolescence and manhood. Masculinity is not seen as an innate state but as something that needs to be transmitted from an older male, and boys and teenagers would be required to fellate or be penetrated by them for periods of up to a year, before being allowed to penetrate women or enter the marriage circuit. In some cultures, male–male sexual activities may continue after this period has ended, whereas in others they tend not to. But crucially, engaging in these practices was not considered socially proscribed within the group itself – even if for individuals it may have been a source of pain and trauma – and potency could be understood as a gift or transmission from an older male, via their semen.

When I was fact-checking this book to see if the early anthropological studies of these male initiation rituals had been revised or updated, I found myself being constantly rerouted to 'Iron John'-type websites, which invoked the indigenous practices as part of their own mythology. The emphasis on anal penetration was played down here in favour of the segregation from women, the ingestion of semen and the idea that manhood requires the intervention of an older, more powerful male agent. The anthropologists themselves note a decline in ritual initiation, and its redrafting and softening using elements of imported religion and culture.

And yet the possibility of bodily penetration is absolutely current in Western societies which do not subscribe to such ritual practices, and we could think of the thousands of jokes and rhymes which make anal penetration a real prospect. A series of once popular jokes start with a landscape emptied of females: the mining town in the American West. Then, to distance the content of the joke so that it is not too anxiety-provoking, racial stereotypes are introduced. To make sure that the tellers and listeners aren't immediately represented in the joke – so to keep the necessary distance – the stereotypes function to say, 'It's not me, it's them.'

Let's take two examples. In the first, a man arrives in a mining town and enquires at the saloon what he can do for sex in the apparent absence of any women. The bartender says, 'Well, you can use the [racial stereotype] out back.' The man is uneasy and says, 'Well, will anyone know?' The bartender replies, 'Oh, don't worry, only the five of us.' The man says, 'What do you mean, five of us?', to which the bartender replies, 'Well, you'll know, and I'll know and the [racial stereotype] will know.' 'But that makes three, not five. Who are the other two?' 'Oh,' says the bartender, 'that'll be the two holding the [racial stereotype] down.' The joke shows that things can be even worse than being a degraded sexual object: one can be physically forced into this role.

In a second variant, the man asks the bartender what he can do for sex, who replies, 'Well, there's the barrel out back with the [racial stereotype] in it.' He's again uneasy and is reassured by the bartender that this is quite normal for the town. 'Yes,' he explains, 'you can do it every day except Wednesday.' 'Why not Wednesday?' the man asks. 'Because that's your turn in the barrel.' This second joke brings out the truth of the first: that the person being penetrated is the man himself, and, by identification, the teller and listener of the joke. The place of being the sexual object of another man – which is part of the ritual ascension to manhood in many cultures – is here the point of the most acute terror. If sexual orientations are the products of fear, perhaps some male heterosexuality is driven by this terror, whereas those who are unpersuaded by heterosexuality may be less troubled by this.

*

Heterosexualities here are of course just as much a product of a complex conflict of forces as homo-sexualities. In his famous coming-out piece in the *New York Times* in 1971, Merle Miller quoted the psychiatrist Martin Hoffman on this: 'Heterosexual behaviour is as much a scientific puzzle as homo-sexual behaviour. We assume that heterosexual arousal is somehow natural and needs no explan-ation' but 'to call it natural is to evade the whole issue: it's as if we said it's natural for the sun to come up in the morning and left it at that.' Neither set of sexual orientations can be seen as the simple result of some childhood experience – a doting mother, a distant father, a traumatic seduction, etc. – and the real question here is why we would seek to find a single 'cause' in the first place. As Gagnon and Simon observed, the patterns of heterosexual-ity and homosexuality are consequent upon the social structures and values that surround the person once they conceive of themselves as hetero-sexual or homosexual, rather than on some ultimate and original biological or psychological mandate.

Homosexualities – like heterosexualities – should be in the plural here, since there is no single entity that the terms refer to, and one of the key efforts of American sociologists in the 1960s and 70s was to suggest that heterosexualities were just as much a product of cultural conditioning as any other form of sexual orientation. Margaret Mead had already argued in the 1940s that heterosexuality was a cultural construction, and later the sex activist and artist Betty Dodson had even proposed a 'Het Pride' rally, not to condone the heterosexist ideologies that she fought so vigorously against but to suggest that heterosexuality was in dire need of accounting for and deconstructing its apparent practices.

There was a widespread questioning here of the assumption that heterosexuality had a life of its own that did not require unpacking and explaining, and of the use of sexual practice to shape imagery of 'the homosexual', as if what people did with their bodies determined all aspects of their lives. Sex practices, they argued, are consequences rather than causes of homosexual orientations, and human lives could hardly be defined by who one slept with. It was often pointed out that terms like 'hetero' and homo' designated forms of love rather than sexual identities, and hence had a flexibility across all genders, but this emphasis risked sapping the political dimension of the debate, which aimed at rights and recognitions.

Fighting against stigmatization at all levels of society required forms of solidarity and the creation of 'communities', even if individuals may well have felt their difference from the collective voice they were supposed to hold. 'Basing your identity on sexuality is like building a house on a foundation of pudding,' wrote gender activist and educator D. Travers Scott, yet consolidating identities seemed necessary to many for political change. Leverage and progress here meant saying 'We' and not simply 'I', and then finding a way out of the fallout afterwards. 'I don't want to be identified,' Scott continues, 'named, pinned down, understood. Those are all the first steps to manipulation and control,' even if for others this may in itself constitute a liberating experience. The challenge for many was — and still is — to empower a political voice that can include difference within it.

This pluralization is echoed today in the expansion of gender labels that has generated so much debate. In the 1960s, it was often said that under-represented and stigmatized minority groups were awaiting their 'verb', while today it is perhaps less a verb than a noun. Working with children, I have found that many are terrified of identifying with the labels 'cis' or 'het' as this is seen as conventional or just plain bad. There are huge social pressures in some segments of society to assume specific gender labels and this is reinforced by the child and adolescent's well-known sense of 'difference'. Each child feels like an outsider, and may seek social roles – and labels – that organize this sense of difference and make it meaningful.

When we hear young people saying that they were born in the wrong body, this can be both a sign of the general human impossibility of inhabiting one's body or of a conviction about gender, but also an effect of social forces. Some children, indeed, are very concerned about what they are *not*, and will go to great lengths to differentiate themselves from labels and certain social roles through acts of rejection, even if they may be less sure about who or what they actually *are*. This can generate a cycle of gravitation away from and then towards labels, especially those that seem to name the gravitation away.

Negotiating social forces here is hardly an easy task. From the late 1960s onwards, a privileged way for a non-cis-identified person to be heard was to say something like 'I've always felt like X' or 'I've always known I was Y', and while there are of course many people who have had this experience, for others it is a language necessary to gain access to recognition and services. As trans activist Miquel Missé points out, such seemingly monolithic views can hide more subtle and complex relations to gender, which the person may find even more difficult to articulate in a society that actually wants everyone to know categorically who they are. There's really not much space – if any – for someone to explore what lies in between a surface affirmation of certainty regarding gender and what may be a deeper ambiguity.

Significantly, when Ronald and Juliette Goldman finished their vast study of children's conceptions of sexuality, they found that the most perplexing question for youngsters was less 'Where do babies come from?' or 'What is sex?' than 'How is it decided whether it's a boy or a girl?' This dilemma was totally absent from Freud's radar, and generally fails to appear in psychoanalytic studies of the sexual theories of childhood. Yet the Goldmans concluded that this was the single most mysterious and unsolvable issue, which must in turn have effects on the way that children later position themselves in terms of gender labels.

Writing on the gender question just after the Second World War, and in the wake of *Fortune* magazine's poll result that 3.3 per cent of American men would rather be born again as women, Margaret Mead argued that the inevitable rejections and frustrations in the life of every child must, at some point, become linked to the gender expectation of parents. Whether there was the wholesale belief 'I was only an accident' or 'I wasn't wanted', or more subtle feelings of disappointing a parent in some way, this may become fused with the idea 'I wasn't the sex they wanted'. Not every child, Mead observes, has the security to say, as a girl did after learning that her mother had wanted twins, 'Oh, I wanted to be twins, but I couldn't be twins, so I just ordered me.'

In terms of the question of sexuality, however, there is a hiatus – widely recognized today – between sexual identity and sexual practice. The question of who we are – the gender label – might promise to tell us what we should do and feel and with whom, in a sexual encounter, but scripts here may stop short of this or explicitly abdicate responsibility. Such separations, however, when they occur, between sexual identity and sexual orientation, are rarely hermetic, and people are left with expectations, unanswered questions, dilemmas and fears, as the questions 'Who am I?' and 'What should I do?' jostle with each other and fail to coalesce. When they do converge, it is often when we imagine other people's sexuality rather than our own.

In terms of sexual practice, it is quite striking how Western heterosexual men tend to imagine that gay men's activity of choice is anal inter-course, when this is statistically less frequent than other forms of sexual intimacy, such as fellatio and mutual masturbation (though this has obvi-ously varied a great deal geographically and historically). Similarly, hetero men tend to think that gay women insert objects into each other's vaginas as a matter of course, when, again, this is less common than vulval stimulation. Note how even the use of dildoes in female-to-female sex was once described as 'using a dildo to' or 'on' rather than 'in' the other person.

It has been estimated that for every represen-tation of a man and woman copulating in European erotic art up to the mid twentieth cen-tury, there was one of two women having sex, and, as Lord Kennet pointed out, the absurd fre-quency with which male writers and artists depict women using dildoes with each other is a desperate attempt to convince everyone of the importance of the phallus, and to prove that women desire just like men. The people who really do put stuff inside themselves are the little boys, who so frequently have experimented as

children by inserting fruit, vegetables and bathroom objects into their rectum.

The key question here is whether these beliefs
and practices involve an ascription of a male–
female penetration to all parties – so that what
same-sex couples do together is presumed to be just
like what het men and women do – or, on the contrary, if even the idea of male–female penetration is
an encrypted representation of male–male penetration. The first of these interpretations was once
pervasive in many areas of the women's movement,
which branded butch–femme couples as unsavoury
replicas of male–female gender stereotypes. But
these heterosexual stereotypes may, indeed, already
include defences against the threat of male penetration. We could think here of the many stories and
rhymes, omnipresent in popular culture since the
early modern period, in which a man penetrating
someone else's wife is surprised from behind by the
husband, who in turn penetrates him, either ration-
alized as a punishment or as an escalation of
pleasure.

In a Lesu myth of the origin of coitus, a medicine man places the male party of the primal

couple into position, and then pushes a burning root into his anus, which then propels him to penetrate the female partner. Heterosexual intercourse here is based on a male–male sexual act, and, as we have seen, the desire to penetrate may often be a treatment of the mixture of anxieties and wishes around being penetrated. These acts could also be understood as a version of the initiation rituals we discussed earlier, in which one man's potency depends on some sort of phallic gift from another man, but it is also worth considering if these two explanations are actually one and the same. That the fear of being penetrated and the idea of initiation into masculinity are two sides of the same coin, with the penis always requiring some input from the older man, even if the idea of 'input' can be terrifying if construed in a literal bodily sense. Curiously, experiments in psychology from the 1950s on that aimed to measure anxiety would often show subjects films of the ritual incision of the penis, as if what was a norm in one culture would be the measure of horror in the other.

Anxiety here may be shifted away from the

penis, as if the vagina is in itself a more terrifying structure. Let's take the *Alien* films again as an example. In this hugely successful franchise, the iconic creature's jaws extend outwards from its head in order to devour its prey, an image that is almost always interpreted as feminine: the female sex, the devouring mother, etc. But isn't the most obvious thing about this image its homology with the glans penis, as the foreskin is retracted from the head? The mechanics of this process can be incredibly disturbing to boys, as can the many worries about something going wrong, from infection to calcification to lesion. John Ruskin famously ran out of the bedroom on his wedding night as the sight of his bride's sex was unbearable to him, yet the image of the corona, glans and foreskin can be equally unsettling.

The removal of the foreskin, so widespread globally and sanctioned by major religions, perhaps reduces this terror, and has two other important functions. Historically, it incarnates sacrifice, as a part of the body is given up to secure the benevolence of the god, or at least the temporary refuge from divine wrath. The penis – or part of it – is always circumcised *for* someone else in religious narratives. The stone phalli that would adorn household perimeters in classical Greece were there less to scare off burglars than as symbols of appeasement, offerings to persuade the gods, and it is interesting to see this as a fundamental feature of the phallus.

When heavy stone phalli were found in the knapsacks of First World War troops, there was puzzlement that such unwieldy objects had been transported so diligently in dangerous conditions. Were they intended for jest – 'just for laughs' according to one wounded soldier – or as tools for perpetrating violence on captured women or for homoerotic use? None of these explanations seemed plausible at the time, and yet whatever rationalizations can be marshalled here their function as talismans would seem probable, especially given the broader sacrificial context of trench warfare in which young men are dispatched to almost certain death by older ones. The phallus is there, perhaps, to ward off fate.

Although there are still today cults of phallic worshippers – I met one recently who explained without any irony her ritual adoration of the male penis – the phallus is less what we sacrifice *to* than what we use *to* sacrifice. It is thus always linked to some other, external and more powerful agency, whether we see this as a deity or an impersonal force like chance or destiny. If the phallus has at times been identified with a symbol of power, beneath this is its more fundamental status as the sign of a lack of power.

The second function of circumcision is to regulate sexual jealousy in the family. A father described how at the moment of his son's circumcision he at last understood what this strange ritual was really about: it meant that he would never have to feel threatened by his son. The cutting of the penis would ensure that nothing bad would happen, that the son was wounded once and for all, and this dialectical dimension is clear in the way that in some cultures the father cannot have sex with the mother until the son's wound has healed. In jokes, indeed, as Legman noticed, castration is always represented as a revenge punishment.

The field of sexual jealousy is nicely set out in

the vignette told of Sir Walter Raleigh and his son, usually censored from editions of John Aubrey's *Brief Lives*. The son is seated next to his father at a banquet, and tells him that earlier that day he 'went to a whore. I was very eager of her, kissed and embraced her, and went to enjoy her, but she thrust me away from her, and vowed I should not, "for your father lay with me just an hour ago".' Sir Walter, on hearing this, 'put out of his countenance at so great a table', struck him violently, and his son, choosing not to return the blow directly, struck the person sitting on his other side, with the hope: 'Box about: 'twill come to my father anon.'

Where psychoanalysis had first emphasized the son's hostility to the father, in the well-known parricidal wishes of the Oedipus complex, the latter's own ambivalence to the son later became clear. Indeed, the negative feelings towards the male child are hardly suppressed in the many parenting manuals for fathers published in the late nineteenth and early twentieth century, which have been described as 'absolutely open hostility'. If circumcision is, in part, a way of treating this, we might wonder about the psychological and social effects of 'reskinning', the common operation in antiquity and beyond which would undo the effects of circumcision, and there was a substantial classical literature on the different varieties and techniques available.

Simple removal of the foreskin, indeed, left the corona capped by the vestigial rim of the preputial membrane, which would eventually retract to reveal an angular scar which could be incised for reskinning. Talmudic circumcision, however, aimed to rule out this possibility by resecting the frenulum, the band of tissue that contracts the foreskin over the glans, uncapping the corona and forming a fleshy scar which could not be made to disappear. Even today, each new pope has to be checked to make sure they have not been 'reskinned' and demonstrate definitively that they have not been circumcised.

These historical and psychological perspectives suggest that the penis is hardly a weapon, but rather something under threat and certainly vulnerable. Weaponizing then takes on a defensive quality, as if the very instrument that is open to attack is used to attack. Wartime sexual assaults so often involve not just the rape, violation and then murder of girls and women but the post-mortem insertion of a penis-like object into the vagina: a bottle or stick. The phallic aspect of the attack has to be emphasized here, as if the penis itself is not enough to do this, and participants in gang or group assaults usually have to mastur-bate in order to maintain erection.

Many studies of arousal and erection have found, indeed, that fear of attack correlates more closely with sexual excitement than attacking itself. These usually involved showing a porn film to a group of men after having exposed them to some horrific images of bodily mutilation, but the range of 'stimuli' chosen did not stop there. In one of the most absurd studies, male subjects were instructed to cross two bridges in Canada: the first a solid well-built structure, the second a narrow wobbly suspension bridge. As they crossed, they were met by a female student – categorized as conventionally 'attractive' – who asked them to fill out a questionnaire. She then supplied each man with her phone number, offering to explain the project in more detail. The researchers found that far more men who crossed the scary suspension bridge called than those who went across the solid structure.

The conclusion was that fear may contribute to arousal, but the symbolism of the bridges presumably eluded the experimenters: one solid and standing proud, the other risking collapse. This tells us more about the researchers than about the experiment's subjects, and it is perhaps not surprising that the female student's subjectivity was also totally deleted from the experimental data: what, after all, might she have felt to be on a scary precarious bridge, having to engage with a group of men she didn't know, and how might her feelings then have been expressed – subliminally or not – to the male subjects?

*

The debates around fellatio are illuminating here, as it was a very serious philosophical question in the classical world to determine how a man receiving a blow job should conduct himself, as it was implicitly construed as a point of vulnerability. Should he stay still? Should he use his hands? Was speaking permitted? Fellatio was distinguished from irrumation, in which the fellator was passive and the man being fellated would vigorously move his penis in and out of the other person's mouth in a coital motion. In fellatio as such, the man being fellated would remain more or less stationary and not move his penis, while the fellator would be active.

Imagine if philosophy courses today reintroduced this, driven not only by the historical pedigree of the subject but by the amount of strife caused in couples by men's insistence on fellatio, and the fact that receiving it tops lists of male phantasy requirements. It is also the sexual practice of choice for men who visit prostitutes (alongside talking), always scoring much higher than penetrative sex. The old explanation for men's quite extraordinary taste for blow jobs was that it allowed an avoidance of the woman's sex, as the vagina was believed unconsciously to contain teeth that could cut into the penis: the famous *vagina dentata*. But this is belied by the fact that in fellatio the penis is being put into the one part of the woman's body that really does have teeth. The technique is favoured by many sex workers, as it renders the sexual encounter significantly shorter and involves less exposure of the rest of the body. So why is it so popular with men?

Presidents Félix Faure and F. D. Roosevelt were even said to have passed away while receiving a blow job ('sitting for a portrait'), and it is seriously depicted as the acme of a man's sexual pleasure. Another analytic explanation took as its starting point the vocabulary of fellatio: it is often described as sucking the penis, when the actual physical actions do not generally involve sucking, which could lead to injury. The many boys who experiment with self-fellating often discover this to their surprise and discomfort, confusing suction with buccal friction. What we do suck as infants is of course the breast, and so it seemed to some psychoanalysts that blow jobs involve an equation of the penis with the nipple. Just as we were once dependent on milk flowing out of a nipple or teat, so we then invert this by becoming the dispenser of a whitish bodily fluid ourselves.

In other words, we become the active agent of the very process that we were once in an enslaved, passive relation to. Irrumation, indeed, is from the Latin *irrumare*, to give suck, as a mother gives the nipple to her nursing child.

We could note here how teenage het boys often describe early sexual contacts as accomplishments in which they 'get all they can' out of a girl, as if she is a breast to be drained. If she fails to yield, she is punished, but she is also punished if she yields – remember witch-dunking? – in the slut-shaming that is so pervasive in male and female social groups. Taken to its logical extreme, the oral relation is reversed, so that in the blow job, at one level, men become what once had power over them, and at another there is arguably a component of revenge and not simply mastery at play here: 'I can give you milk and then drop you.' Karen Horney thought that revenge was probably the single most important factor in psychical life, a remarkable observation given its almost complete absence from analytic theory. To follow this thinking through, it might then suggest that if the penis in fellatio is inverting a power relation, so is the penetrative sex act itself: just as we all exited a body forcefully when we were born, so now we push our way back in forcefully. Coitus in this sense involves an act of vengeance, and it would illuminate both male and female phantasies of self-insertion into someone else's body.

The violent thrusting that many men see as the central dynamic of the sexual act thus becomes an inversion of the thrusting-out that permitted their very birth. And combined with this, in the violence, is a vengeance for every wrong the mother ever perpetrated and all the power she once held over him. Sex for a man might thus be a sort of miracle! He manages both to become his mother and take revenge on her. What more could he want?

*

This convergence of becoming the mother and taking revenge on her may shed light on the popular practice of 'facials'. This refers to the man ejaculating in a woman's face, and was famously touted by Britain's much-loved rap artist Stormzy, who boasts of finishing off his sex act by giving his partner a facial in the song 'Vossi Bop'. The fact that – like the Rolling Stones' regrettable treatment of sexual violence 'Midnight Rambler' – this was widely played on UK radio and even nominated for an award testifies to the strange double standards that operate in our culture: what we condemn at one level we adulate under the disguise of art in another.

The real question here, of course, is why so many het men do this to women whereas it is much rarer in gay hook-ups or relationships. A man is doing this to a woman, but a gay man apparently feels less compelled to do this to another man (although male–male urination is hardly a rarity). The gendering here suggests that beyond the manifest humiliation – what Gayle Rubin calls 'erotic injustice' – is the reminder to the woman that the man has got white fluid too, and that he is the one who can control, dispense and withhold it. The delighted, involuntary laughter that men sometimes report afterwards perhaps expresses a sense of triumph and victory.

It is interesting here to compare the place of the ejaculation in traditional male and female prostitution. The female prostitute is usually paid for the man's ejaculation whereas the male prostitute – until relatively recently in some parts of the world – for his own ejaculation. Female prostitutes are aware of the man's wish to debase her with semen – and hence the well-known acronyms such as CIF (cum in face) or COB (cum on body) to refer to non-vaginal deposits of semen. There is no acronym, as far as I know, for coming into a condom (CIC?). In pornography, too, the act of penetrative sex is practically never completed inside a woman's body but only when the man ejaculates on to her. If we followed the equation of semen with milk, this may suggest the variety of positions that a child might seek: to be the supplier oneself, or to have the power to create the supply, or to withhold it.

An escort in analysis explained that for her facials were not a problem in themselves, as they generally meant that she was not obliged to swallow male semen, but that the real danger was if the man 'won'. When I asked what this referred to, she said that if the man shot his semen into her eye it would mean he had won, an expression that, through a chain of association, led to the idea of impregnation via the eye. Absurd and irrational, she admitted, but nonetheless powerfully present in her mind whenever a client proposed a facial: the male ejaculate could enter via the ocular aperture, planting a seed inside her.

Curiously, the very idea of 'winning' is in many societies linked to an ejaculatory display. Think of what happens after a Formula One race. The winning driver shakes a magnum of champagne and sprays it over their team. The symbolism here is perhaps self-evident, but I suppose it is a question whether the group are being urinated over or ejaculated over. We could compare this with the breaking of the actual bottle of champagne when a ship is launched: invariably feminine, the ship is 'broken in' with an obvious symbolism of a breach of the hymen.

Without wishing to affect the champagne market in either a positive or a negative way, the genealogy of the refined erotic act of drinking champagne from a woman's shoe is worth mentioning here. Sometimes seen as the height of a classy debauchery, it derives from the occasional Elizabethan practice of drinking from the chamber pot of a courted woman. When Hamlet probes the extent of Laertes' love for his sister, asking him, 'Wilt drink up vessels?' in the First Quarto version, this is what he means, and the beverage would move from urine to bathwater to champagne, finally, in the nineteenth century.

Both boys and girls in early childhood may try to mouth the urinary jet of their father when he is peeing, and boys later often compete with each other as to who can pee furthest and for longest. When they are able to produce semen, this also becomes the object of comparison in the traumatic bull parties of adolescence with their 'circle jerks' and 'chain jerks': who can ejaculate the furthest? Who can come fastest? Later on, of course, the premium will shift from haste to delay, as men worry about their ejaculatory latencies: how long will they be able to have sex without coming? The continuity of concern here about urine and semen shows the importance of the male homosocial group for how the penis is valued: they are both the judges and the competitors.

The facial may also have this homosocial dimension, linking the man to a group of men who do it too, bonded together by their mutual debasing of women. The other, more obvious feature of this sexual practice is its exhibitionistic aspect. The penis is revealed and displayed, and its potency demonstrated. This will occur presumably at those moments when, precisely, the person feels most under threat and vulnerable, something which is clear when exhibitionistic acts take place in public. So-called exhibitionists fall into two groups: those who display their penis at a time of great duress to some sort of depersonalized audience – such as passengers on a passing train – and those who breach boundaried spaces to show their penis to a single person, with the aim of causing them anxiety.

There are totally different motivations at play here. In the former group, the person seeks a sanction, a registration of his penis, and has no wish to harm his audience. The requirement of a symbolic abstract registration is reflected in the fact that the audience is depersonalized, often a crowd or series of people who can't be differentiated. In the latter group, the exhibitionist does seek to have a specific effect on his very particular victim, to cause her division, anxiety, loss of composure, and such acts may be followed later on by acts of physical violence. In the former group, it's the penis that matters; in the latter, it's the victim. When legal agencies treat these two groups as equivalent, they fail to recognize significant risk factors.

*

Let's say a bit more here about breasts and milk. It's curious how although both boys and girls may be breastfed, the erotic value of the breast and nipple can vary so much. Anthropologists report that in some societies, such as the Mangaians in Polynesia, there was little sexual interest in the breast, and the idea of touching or mouthing it was considered incomprehensible until the arrival of Western media. In other cultures where the breast does have a privileged erotic valence, many women have no real interest in having their breasts manipulated by a clumsy man, whereas others may be intensely aroused as their breasts are pressed and pummelled. For some, the sexual value of the breast is a direct function of their partner's excitement, showing how what makes an erogenous zone may depend on the way someone else perceives it.

Women often complain of men's lack of sensitivity here, no doubt sensing the violence in the fondling action, as if a subtle kind of revenge is at play on the woman's body. The breast that once had power over him is being punished: it's payback time. No more dependency. The very long history of wartime mutilations and excisions of the breasts of girls and women in 'enemy' territory, stretching from classical times until today, shows this in its most extreme form, but the motifs of violence are omnipresent culturally.

Reading through Gustave Witkowski's four-volume history of the breast is a sad and upsetting experience, as it is in many ways just a catalogue of acts of violence against women, whether explicit or disguised. The adorative paeans to this part of the female body in the Renaissance verse genre of *blasons* are matched by the invective of the *counterblasons*, in which each positive statement is matched by an insult, and motifs of possession and hostility are ubiquitous. In Jack Litewka's account of the sexual script of his generation, 'you begin to attack the flesh of the breast' before continuing on to 'the rainbow's gold – the assault on the nipple'. The language is quite unambiguous, and we could also think here of the old pornographic currency of cellophane packets of photos depicting simply the act of breast-kneading.

But as well as painful manipulation, men also have another important agenda as they touch and mouth a nipple: to make it erect. Post-war Western culture put a premium, indeed, on breasts that were actually pointing upwards like a phallus, and even came up with a military name for these inventions: howitzers. Pendant breasts risked making men uncomfortable, and it is difficult not to see in this an equation between breast, nipple and penis, as if the man is reassuring himself not only that a woman has some kind of phallic feature but that he has the capability to generate the erection. What men do with the nipple, indeed, is often more exciting for them than it is for the woman.

In a recent advert for Mazda cars, a male driver is transporting some female mannequins and is obviously enjoying his ride. When he reaches his destination and stops the car, visibly elated, we see that the mannequins have now all got erect nipples. This ad is a quite precise representation of much male sexuality: the man would rather be driving than with a woman, the women in his life are reduced to lifeless silent mannequins, and their arousal is the same as his arousal, conceived phallically as erection. Female excitement is male excitement.

This kind of equation might clarify the unease many people have around the idea of female ejaculation. If men want women to enjoy just like them – in an effort to negate difference – surely their ejaculation would be acceptable, and indeed, until about 120 years ago, it formed a standard part of pornographic descriptions of male–female sex acts. Women would emit a fluid just like men.

Ovid had noted his preference for sex with 'girls' due precisely to 'the simultaneous ejaculation of both parties', and erotic literature is full of references to female 'liquid', 'rivers', 'fountains' and 'streams'. But this would later become pathologized or simply denied, and medical authorities could state well into the twentieth century that female ejaculation just didn't exist. Liquid emissions would be explained away as excessive perspiration or urinary incontinence, but even once this had been disproved, researchers were still left with the problem of where such a quantity of fluid could have been stored, if the bladder was excluded.

While female ejaculation is recognized today as an authentic phenomenon, it still has for many an aura of mystery and taboo, and often carries a sense of shame, as if it somehow dirties the sex act, although for others it is a valued asset. At a more unconscious level, it may be actively sought out as it confirms a parity of phallic-style sexuality, or avoided and denied for this same reason: the idea that a woman has an ejaculatory organ and capacity is felt as too anxiety-provoking. It may also be disturbing because it implies that a woman still has liquid to dispense and not just the man, so effectively cancelling the temporary identification of penis and breast.

Yet this equation of breast and penis can work both ways. Women may describe phantasies – and sometimes practices – of inserting their breast into another woman's vagina, or being themselves penetrated by an elongated breast. This was perhaps most famously evoked in the letters served as evidence in the Lord and Lady Cavendish divorce trial in 1865, where her lover writes of 'the fear you have lest I should fetch a young girl to violate you with her breasts in your cunt', before describing his own inflated penis. Both penis and breast here are organs to be incorporated or to penetrate with, and it must be one of the tasks of every child to somehow process the question of the relation between these two active body parts. We start life, after all, being penetrated by a part of someone else's body that spurts milk into us. We soon learn that a penis spurts urine, and, perhaps later, that a penis can enter another body, just as the nipple once did.

It was quite common, indeed, in the eighteenth and nineteenth centuries, for European dildoes to be filled with warm milk, and the pornography of the time often makes comparisons with the breastfeeding infant. The liquid is to be sucked or received internally as a baby sucks the nipple, and it could be released at the appropriate moment either through squeezing the base of the dildo or through more complex spring mechanisms. Preparing the milk and readying the device for use was referred to as 'charging' the dildo, just as we use the term today for our phones and laptops. Penis and breast are identified here rather than separated.

If this equation remains at the level of an identity, sexuality stays oral. The basic mechanisms of mouthing will structure all other bodily processes during sex – incorporating, swallowing, ingesting, spitting out – with a greater or lesser importance accorded to each depending on the particular person. Analysts had noticed many years ago how the archaic actions and properties of the mouth may be displaced to the vagina, urethra and vulva to create a kind of sexual grammar: opening and closing, retaining and expelling, ingesting and spitting out could govern the sexual organs just as they did the oral cavity. And hence the many forms of oral sexuality – refusal to eat, bingeing, etc. – could create their own effects at a genital level. As Selma Fraiberg put it, oral symptomology can 'provide the vocabulary for the genitals'. Some argued that, indeed, the vagina actually required this transfer of properties in order to come to life, as the vital sexuality of the mouth innervated the rest of the body.

Eating and being eaten are well-known experiences in sex, just as hunger is one of the most common descriptors of sexual arousal and desire. At times, there is the wish to bite into and incorporate the other person's body, and also to actually swallow them whole. Initially understood by many analysts as an act of sadism or aggression, Freud thought that this did not necessarily entail a hostile intention, but could be seen simply as a form of love. This observation is echoed in the distinction between sexual cannibalism and 'vorarephilia'. There are online communities today devoted to the exploration of 'vore', the phantasy of either swallowing someone whole or being swallowed whole, and there are often requests that posted phantasies ban the inclusion of chewing. Trigger warning – chewing!

Presumably this would damage the person being swallowed, showing how love and preservation may be more important than destruction. It is interesting to note that if swallowing is primarily invited through the mouth, it can also occur, in vore phantasies, through the vagina, the anus or the breasts, suggesting the action of oral grammar on the rest of the body. Pregnancy motifs are ubiquitous here, with people describing their wish to be held and contained in the belly of the swallower, evoking the 'sexual theory' of childhood in which a baby is the result of ingestion.

An analysand described her difficulty in leaving a lover who, she felt, was not right for her, but the sexual dynamic between them 'was just too strong'. The other woman would quite literally 'devour' her, sucking and pulling with her mouth at every part of her body, as if she had to be taken in and consumed in a kind of

Darian Leader

'feeding frenzy'. She linked this to her curious fascination with the film *Anaconda* – totally at odds with her otherwise highbrow taste in art cinema – in which characters are swallowed whole by an abnormally large snake. When anxious, she would watch this film again and again, finding the scenes of ingestion strangely comforting. 'My friends watch *Friends* when they're upset,' she said, 'but I watch *Anaconda*.'

It is perhaps unsurprising, given all these associations, that sex, like feeding, may end in sleep, although things are actually a bit more complicated here. We often assume that babies fall asleep after their feed, but although this is sometimes true, there is very often a crucial time interval in which mother and baby play with each other, with their hands, voices, eyes and all the other possibilities of interaction available to them. If sleep follows immediately, some infant researchers have argued that this is not an effect of satiation but to avoid the intense sensory stimulation of breast or bottle feeding.

If we applied this model to sex, sleep would

be a defence mechanism, a way of absenting one-self and perhaps avoiding the conversation that many people feel must follow the sexual act. Lacan even suggested that the origin of human language is here: not in the guttural cries of workers in some field or hunters chasing their prey, but in the awkward silence that follows ejaculation. 'Was that good for you?'

*

Gagnon and Simon point out that most people don't know how to talk about sex, even with people they are having sex with. In pornography, male actors are hardly verbose, and usually stay silent, unless to insult their partner or greet a third party. We tend to associate the decline in the capacity to speak with an increase in sexual excite-ment, so that verbal exchanges become limited. Interestingly, as sex scenes in fiction and main-stream cinema became raunchier, communication after sex declined, going from some 89 per cent in the late 1950s to 55 per cent by the end of the 70s.

This inverse proportion between speech and

pleasure is famously applied today to the whole issue of consent, as consent requests are felt to dampen arousal. We should just be moaning, sighing and expressing excitement rather than asking for agreement or permission. Today there are apps and even contracts for consent, as if this would somehow resolve the question, yet someone may change their mind before, during or after sex, for a variety of reasons. The first sex scene between Marianne and Connell in *Normal People* touched millions of readers – and viewers of the TV series – as consent and consideration became part of the 'flow' of the sex rather than some external interruption. Yet after this instructive opening, the issue of consent became much more complicated once the question of Marianne's interest in violence and pain was foregrounded.

Although consent and violence tend to be perceived as polarities, consent itself can be an effect of violence. Most adults around the world who work to maintain basic sustenance don't exactly have much of a choice to consent to any aspect of their lives, and this will include sex as well. Women living in violent relationships report low levels of sexual arousal and satisfaction, yet have sex much more often than those who do not describe physical abuse. Coercion here is the rule, and refusing consent is clearly not felt to be an option for a very large number of women worldwide. According to one study, 14 per cent of American women are forced to have sex against their will, whereas this figure rises to 40 per cent with battered women.

In affluent sectors of Western society, consent is heralded as an expression of agency, yet the widely publicized idea of being the author of one's own life is largely fantastical. Agency itself is shaped by social conditions, and the voguish idea of self-authorship is a recognized product of late capitalism, in which people are enjoined to make their own lives in conditions which effectively disallow this. But even if we go beyond the rhetoric of autonomy, most of us say Yes when we would rather say No, as the pandemic showed very clearly: it was no longer necessary to come up with excuses for not doing things as we simply were not allowed to. The state said No for us.

In the highly charged and potentially intimate

situation of a sexual encounter, there may be even more pressure to consent to things we have no desire to do, for similar reasons. This might mean a Yes, but also a No if there is a conflict between who we want to please most. Actress Dyan Cannon recalls her intense excitement and desire to continue with her lovers being interrupted when she thought of her bond to her parents. She wanted to say Yes: 'But I did say No because it was more important to please Mummy and Daddy.'

As children, we learn to associate submission and agreement with the receipt of love: if we do what we're told, our parents won't withdraw their love and reject us. So if you want someone to love – or like – you, better do what they tell you. The flip side of this is that if we somehow succeed in going beyond the wish to be loved, and pursue only what we find pleasurable, we risk becoming the very thing that is so culturally deplored: the selfish lover only interested in their own satisfaction. Or, to put it another way, the very person we should be saying No to.

There are obviously gradations here – and we

could introduce categories such as empathy or respect for the other – but beyond these is often the uncomfortable childhood reality of feeling that we can only be accepted if we agree with the adult's judgement and evaluation of us. And this creates the paradoxical situation that to feel loved, we must be at some level helpless or worthless. Many of these issues are treated in BDSM practices, through the use of protocols of agreement and trust which provide temporary conventionalized strategies for dealing with requests and consent, as well as helplessness.

It is curious how BDSM seems to be the most robust way of navigating the basic issues here, as if what is taken to be a marginal set of sexual practices should in fact be the 'gold standard' in matters of agency. When push comes to shove, there can of course be boundary violations and unexpected violence in BDSM, but it gives a nice image of rule-bound practice to those who are uneasy about what the rules of sex might be, or whether there are indeed any. The psychoanalyst Karin Stephen made the helpful distinction here between acquiescence and consent: we acquiesce

out of fear, but consent when fear is not our mo-
tivating force. Someone can thus say Yes to
plenty of things in sex that they have no desire
to do in order to feel lovable and valued, and this
is arguably a central part of most sexual practice.
But as Amber Hollibaugh points out, 'You can't
truly say Yes until you know that you can say No.'

Take the question of condom use. In some
cultures, even suggesting introducing a condom
is taken to imply that the person or their partner
is diseased or unfaithful, and may trigger real
violence. In other contexts where actual physical
abuse is less likely, if one party requests it, the
other may feel hurt that they are not trusted and
that their body is implicitly felt to be diseased and
dirty. If we feel love for that person, or hope that
they will love us, we might then consent to dis-
pensing with the condom. Love here involves
doing what we might not want to do to please the
other person, which is essentially the story of
most people's childhood. Sadly, therapists are
aware how pervasive lying about sexual health
can be. Someone can genuinely persuade themselves that they are risk-free when this is not the

case, or quite simply lie, and it is an unfortunate fact about sexually transmitted diseases that the best cure for them remains to pass them on to someone else.

This unconscious belief can shape sexual behaviour, even if it generates guilt feelings later on, and it follows the well-known cultural template of Tolkien's ring, an object that brings tragedy to its owners. Myths, folk tales and films represent this way of treating toxicity by transmission: a curse or demonic possession can only be undone if the bewitched object or spirit moves on to someone else. The original malign force cannot in itself be destroyed, but must be displaced, as we see in countless recent films such as *Truth or Dare*, *It Follows*, *Smile* or *Drag Me to Hell*.

*

If we turn now to the detail of sexual practices, we find that psychoanalysts are rather like G. K. Chesterton's drunk who searches for his wallet under a streetlight rather than where he actually lost it. When asked why, he explains it's because that's the only illuminated spot. Perhaps because analysts are supposed to be obsessed with sex, we tend to refrain from asking too much about it, which means that we lose out on a wealth of material that other researchers have accessed. As we are used to hearing people's secrets all day, we assume that we are also being told everything about sex, which is generally not the case.

If an analysand reports having a bad situation at work and returning home to masturbate, the analyst will no doubt ask what happened at work, and probably what they were thinking about while masturbating. This may be significant enough, but we are very unlikely to ask, 'And did you come?', as this would be not only intrusive but also risk setting up some sort of standard the person might feel measured by. Yet the folks who do ask this kind of question find, for example, that an awful lot of people break off their masturbating before orgasm. And also something which analysts have been quite unaware of: that a very large number of people who have a sexual phantasy that they use in masturbation and in sex will suddenly switch to a second and often very different phantasy when they are close to coming.

The role of phantasy in sexual life has often been misunderstood, as if it were somehow a choice between phantasy or sex: we relied on our imagination when we were unable to actually have sex with someone else. Yet analysts and researchers showed that phantasy is less an alternative than a condition: most people need a phantasy to become aroused or to sustain arousal. And we learn how to use phantasy quite early on in life, as we coordinate our daydreams to manipulation of the body. It's quite a feat, after all, to make a significant moment in a story we are picturing coincide with an orgasm. This requires a very complex set of cognitive and physical skills, and it has even been described as a milestone in sensorimotor development, like learning how to write or tie one's shoelaces.

As we learn how to build and use masturbatory stories, we are also learning how to identify with characters, how to be other people, which is arguably something we need in order to read and relate to the world more generally. Phantasy is a profoundly symbolic process, and the way it allows us to be others and shift identities is central to the sexual experience. Men and women are constantly imagining during sex that either they or their partner is someone else, and the most commonly reported phantasies involve identity swaps. Hence the old joke in which a couple are in bed, and one turns to the other, saying, 'How about it?', to receive the reply, 'Sorry, I'm just too tired to think of anyone.'

When we focus here on the need for variety or change as an explanation, we are neglecting the actual symbolic side of the process, the fact that we are turning one person into another. How are we able to do this? And – a crucial question – do we do it anywhere else except in sex? If we are having some sort of disagreement or argument with our boss at work, do we imagine that they are someone else? We might learn to become other people in stories, but does this also mean that we learn how to change one person into another? And to what extent do such processes operate unconsciously, beyond our conscious awareness?

The irony here is that sex is so often taken to be the most intimate moment shared by human beings, a time of real connection, yet it is in fact the one moment when each party is very likely to imagine that their partner is someone else. As they kiss or enter each other's bodies, each person might be imagining that they are kissing or entering someone else. The moment of connection is simultaneously a moment of disconnection.

This might seem surprising, but given the early anxieties and fears we have around bodily boundaries and overproximity, it makes sense that we are always somewhere else when we are so close to another body. This is also almost a requirement of the masturbatory process. As children and adolescents learn to masturbate, they are essentially gaining the skill of following a symbolic mental process while blocking out the awareness that they are touching their genitals. If they were to be aware of both at the same time, the activity would be compromised. For boys, the fact that masturbation ends in ejaculation gives the template of the sexual act, also terminating for them in orgasms (unless they are otherwise educated by their partners). So, the irony once again that the moment of physical connection is made possible by a disconnection.

Sex involves an incredible number of feats of selective attention: we ignore certain sounds and smells while focusing on others, we experience certain bodily feelings while blocking out those we need to avoid, as we move our attention around rapidly. Who is aware, for example, of spasming of the anal sphincter, a sudden rash on the chest or curling of their toes at the moment of orgasm? Rembrandt's erotic print *The Great Bed* gives a nice metaphor of this elision: a youthful couple are having sex on a bed with a vast curtain draped above them. Viewers can stare at this again and again without noticing the most obvious thing about it: the young lady has three arms. Given the artist's rather meticulous care with his plates – burnishing out portions of other works that he was not happy with – it is possible that he intended the print as a comment on precisely how the sexual affects our perception.

Contrary to the popular view that if in phantasy we can cut and paste, in sex we can't, nearly all studies of cognitive processes during sex have found complex patterns of – precisely – cut and paste. As one of Edrita Fried's patients reported, 'The reality of the sex act is not pleasant. Phantasy is better. In phantasy I decide which way things will go,' but phantasy is right there in the sex act itself. We are tuning in and out, and the very sensations we feel hardly flow into each other – as we might like to believe – but often conflict and jar. For Judith Kestenberg, the excitability of the clitoris, urethra, upper and lower vagina, labia and introitus are all of a different order, and this multilocal nature of female arousal can in itself be frightening.

As Ruth Herschberger put it, when we have sex we are running a race and doing geometry at the same time, as 'passion, concern and forbearance' occur simultaneously. Sex for her was a dynamic combination of many different types of experiences linked to multiple sources. Rather than being open to all forms of sensory input – as pop images of sex like to suggest – states of excitation and arousal during sex can block each other, just as we create arousal states such as overwork, nicotine rush or drunkenness in everyday life to block out others, such as grief or vulnerability. We use feelings to control feelings.

This is complicated even further by the fact that we can be in so many places at once. According to the old adage, there are always four people present during sex: the two parties and the lovers they are thinking of at the time. With psychoanalysis, four became at least eight: the two parties, each with a bisexual split within themselves according to Freud, plus both sets of parents. If we add the lovers they are thinking of, that makes ten. And if it's a threesome or an orgy, we need the help of a mathematician. This might sound like a joke, but there are in fact real mathematical problems here that have generated much discussion and debate: given the limited number of apertures on a human body, how can so-called spintrian or daisy chains be organized? Orgies involving more than a certain odd number of participants permutationally must include oral–genital acts, and this becomes even more complex when we factor in personal preferences and sexual orientations.

Even if there are just two people physically

present, each moment in a sexual encounter may be governed by an identification with the other party, as if one is looking through their eyes. It is very frequent for people having sex to imagine that an onlooker is watching – often materializing this external gaze in the form of a mirror – but this onlooker can rapidly switch places with the person themself. An arm, a foot or one's sex may be moved if we feel that the other person may find it somehow unattractive, as if we are in their place as well as our own, judging through their eyes. We might then do something else with our body or theirs to divert attention away from the part we feel uneasy about.

As the body changes and ages, there may be even more pressure to conceal, camouflage or distract, but as we explore the psychology of such situations, we almost always find that the eyes through which we view our own body are ultimately those of someone else: usually a parent whose gaze we have internalized as our own. When we judge a body part as ugly or unappealing, the evaluation carries the shadow of a negative look from a parent, a cutting remark either addressed directly to us or overheard, or even a parent's unabashed effort to change the part in question. Distracting attention from these aspects of the body during sex unfortunately cannot distract from the weight of this negative parental gaze.

These small acts of diversion are ubiquitous during sex, and may involve much more than the visual and tactile perception of the body. The urge to urinate is another example of how a physical process can function to shift attention from other bodily and psychical states. Weeing during sex is in some cultures taken to be a scripted part of female arousal. In one Micronesian population, intercourse can only apparently occur if the woman has urinated during foreplay. In other societies in which it is more or less prohibited, some women are very frightened of it happening, with fears of soiling clothes or bed linen and repelling the partner. The urge to urinate, however, may become necessary to eclipse or divert attention from other internal states, to treat mounting and overwhelming excitements and even the archaic fear of bursting, which is so often evoked when women describe orgasm. Female exploration of the urethra is indeed quite common in childhood, and urethral masturbation has been estimated at around 10 per cent compared to 20 per cent vaginal and 20 per cent via thigh pressure.

Many sexual practices are affected by the childhood fear of bursting or its counterpart, the terror of depletion. These may take the form of images of being pumped full of some substance – presumably stemming from both the experience of being fed and childhood ideas of what parents do to each other – or of being emptied out of everything, linked to the dread of the breast running dry or of the loss of one's viscera. These shadowy fears can become quite explicit in dreams or, more rarely, in sex crimes, but are legible in the most everyday demands for *more* sex, as if bodily intimacy is something that could literally run out. *Fill me up* is indeed a much-clicked rubric on Pornhub.

Excitement itself can be terrifying if the person associates it to these fears, and can shape subtle aspects of sexual practice – how one moves or touches – or cause the avoidance of sex altogether.

Researchers have found that attention moves swiftly from one point to another during sex, shifting from one's own body to the other person's body to phantasy and other thought processes, or even numbers. Some people while pretending to be lost in enjoyment are actually counting silently in their heads. Sensations felt to be wrong or too extreme or repulsive need to be rapidly treated, and so we shut down some levels of awareness and increase others.

The fear of bursting and of losing one's insides might mean that orgasm is carefully sidelined, and the fear of being emptied is often seen in the idea of being cheated that emerges around sexual contacts. There can be the nagging thought that one has actually been robbed of some item, even if the person feels it would be inappropriate to voice this. The thought, nonetheless, persists, generating discord in the relationship, which is often inexplicable to the partner. Interestingly, when we say today that someone has been caught *in flagrante delicto* – meaning in the middle of a sexual act – the expression was originally used to refer to criminals being apprehended in the act of theft.

The tragic boundary between connecting and disconnecting is perhaps clearest after the sexual act itself. The often reported sense of disgust and anger with the other person – usually a woman – may be a consequence of the thought: 'Why aren't you someone else?' A split between idealized love and sexual desire may have allowed arousal to occur in the first place – using the mother/whore dichotomy – but is then followed by all the rage that one has not found what one was really looking for. Cultural images of the ideal woman, which obviously shift historically, can be used as alibis for hatred: the partner has failed to live up to what they are supposed to be.

When Zola finally spent the night with George Sand, after a sustained effort to seduce her, she made no attempt to hide the unchecked nature of her sexual desire. In the morning, Zola left money on the bedside table, as if the reality of her passion disqualified her from the category of 'Woman to be courted', and turned her, instead, into a prostitute.

*

When we explore further the content of phantasies, we find both the strange and the familiar. Men often imagine splitting open a woman's body or driving her unstoppably to orgasm. Male sexual phantasies were traditionally understood as vehicles for power relations, with an active aggressive man and a passive female object, but several later studies from the 1970s on claimed that men were especially attentive in phantasy life to female pleasure, while women, supposedly socialized to pleasure men, in fact focused more on self-pleasuring. The idea that women were only really interested in relationships rather than sex was, as Sallie Tisdale put it, perhaps simply a coded way of saying that this is what they *should* be interested in.

Yet the apparent altruism of the female-sensitive male phantasy may in fact just conceal the old power structure: bringing a woman to orgasm positions the man and his penis in the place of the single active agency, and the orgasm itself can be seen as a form of division, of breaking apart. The man has succeeded in puncturing a woman's self-image, self-restraint, self-composure. So there may be a certain kind of violence hidden in the effort to please the partner. To be able to affect someone deeply, after all, is to have power over them, however temporary.

The vocabulary of orgasm echoes this destructive thread, and it is remarkable to see how, right through the centuries, it is equated with death or a loss of self. In the eighteenth century, it would be common to cry out, 'You kill me!', and orgasm was dubbed 'the little death' in several languages. A study of descriptions of orgasm in contemporary romance novels found that almost half the extracts included images of death, and the ripping, shattering and explosion of bodies. When the Western practice of boxing was introduced into the Cook Islands, the word 'knockout' was swiftly borrowed to describe female orgasm. Loss of boundaries and collapse are frequently evoked: 'I shattered into a million pieces', 'I became atoms and molecules', 'I am lost', 'I'm falling in pieces like a broken plate which would scatter all over', 'a total oblivion', 'a blackout of complete mental awareness'. Although we could of course see in these expressions a lexicon of transcendence – orgasm allowing the person to reach another plane of existence – it is difficult not to also infer a palpable violence, a breaking-apart or disaggregation of bodies.

This is why some people – more women than men – may be cautious and choose to avoid orgasm altogether, as the risks are significant. When researchers found to their astonishment in 1974 that some 7 per cent of female students in New York believed that masturbation could lead to 'insanity', we could interpret this as less a relic of eighteenth- and nineteenth-century medical theories, or the result of poor sex education, than as a realistic assessment of the risks to the sense of self that orgasm might entail. Female fear and male aggression coalesce here at this point of physical and psychical porosity.

The vengeful vector of much male sexuality can also be found in the sequencing of phantasy, and can shed light on the apparently contradict-ory fact that the most frequent male phantasy motifs are sexual power, aggression and . . . masochism. If men so often need phantasies of overpowering and pounding a woman internally with their penis – hardly ever, in the phantasy, against her will – these may be preceded by more passive imagery. So, in order to become aroused and sustain an erection, a man might imagine a woman taking the lead, forcing him to have sex and generally occupying a dominant position. Then, as he becomes more excited and closer to orgasm, this switches to the better-known male dominance phantasy, in which he now becomes the only active agent. Men can speak openly about the second phantasy but much less so about the first, yet the order suggests that the second active part might play out a revenge for the earlier passive sequence.

Fear is probably the key factor here, and Theodor Reik observed many years ago that it is easier for a man to admit being a slave to a woman than to being afraid of her, an avoidance that is reflected in sexual practice. There are plenty of men who pay women to be their masters in domination practices, whereas scenarios in which a man acts out being afraid of a woman are, to my knowledge, rare or non-existent. After seeing thousands of people in his sexology clinic, Claude Crépault could say that he had not once heard a man admit to being afraid of women. Similarly, it is not uncommon for a man to pay a woman to pee or defecate on him, but this is extremely rare – though not totally absent – for women.

The switch in phantasies during sexual acts also questions the well-known disconnection that men seem to show regarding an emotional attachment to their sexual partner. According to the popular cliché, men are supposed to have sex without feeling much whereas women are more likely to have sex when they feel an emotional connection. 'It was only sex' men can say, and may then swiftly move on to the next person. This is usually explained in terms of the mother/whore binary, so popular in nineteenth-century culture and given an Oedipal reading by Freud. Males, he argued, are too disturbed at the proximity of sexual and loving feelings towards the mother, so split them apart: they will desire one woman yet be unable to feel love for her, and love another woman without being able to feel sexual desire for her. Male sexuality, for Freud, was thus a way of managing guilt.

The truth of this explanation seems undeniable, and we see it every day in analytic work. A man might lose sexual desire for his partner the moment she becomes pregnant or takes on some trait associated with the mother, and sexual desire may always gravitate to women who represent 'opposite' traits to her: if the mother is dark, the desired women will be pale, etc. Likewise, a 'pure' maternal image may excite no desire until the man sullies it, debasing and demeaning her with language or action. For some men, they can only come if they insult the woman they are sleeping with, and the feeling of contempt may be a prerequisite to the most basic kind of arousal.

Note how if this splitting is a way of managing guilt, it is also a way of managing meaning. When the man claims to feel nothing for his sexual partner – 'It was just sex' –, this is an operation on meaning: the act did not have any significance for him, and hence can be forgotten, discounted or excused. To love, rather than to desire, in turn confers meaning, suggesting that love and meaning are quite closely connected. On Freud's Oedipal model, if the mother is the primary site of both love and desire, she is also the site of meaning, and so to split love and desire is to split meaning: some partners are felt to mean 'nothing' and others a great deal.

But phantasy life suggests that this categorical separation is never as neat as men would like it to be, and Crépault found that men who used what he calls 'antifusional' scenarios – in which emotion is disconnected and the woman objectified – might suddenly switch to 'fusional' ones – in which a real connection to the woman is felt – as they approach orgasm. As well as indicating the defensive nature of the male mother/whore split, this also sheds light on the sudden distancing and coldness towards women that men often display after ejaculating. The 'fusional' dimension must be negated.

Crépault found a similar bifurcation in female sexual phantasy. Intense feelings of romantic connection during sex might suddenly give way to phantasy images of objectification and absence of attachment just before orgasm. The person might even imagine that the phantasy partner is replaced by an animal, as if to introduce precisely the 'antifusional' dimension that supposedly characterizes male sexual phantasy. 'Most times when we make love,' one woman explains, 'I imagine it is the penis of a large dog or horse that is entering me, or a dog licking me and hordes of dogs all screwing wildly.' It is curious to note here how if women sometimes have phantasies about sex with animals, men practically never do, although they tend, on the contrary, to have phantasies about women having sex with animals.

*

If we turn now to female phantasies, the first thing to recognize is how the early studies of this were misguided. Kinsey and his colleagues thought that female phantasy life was far less pervasive than male's, and that if a man was thinking about some imaginary scenario during sex, a woman was less likely to be doing so. Some psychoanalytic writers held the same view, yet it became quite clear by the 1970s that women phantasize just as much, if not more, than men during sex, though perhaps not at the actual moment of orgasm. These phantasies could change the identity of the partner – or of the woman herself – often anonymizing the other person, rendering them faceless or unclear. Coercion phantasies were also extremely common, and this became a much-discussed topic in the women's movement: was it OK to have rape phantasies, especially if the person having them might actually spend a large part of their life campaigning for women's rights and for changes to male-biased legal and social systems?

The first set of psychological explanations for these phantasies, mostly from therapists, had only been partially and selectively valid. Focusing on heterosexual subjects, they assumed that in the phantasy a man – described as attractive – would be unable to stop himself from overpowering the woman, driven by his passion for her. The rape phantasy was thus, it was argued, a vehicle for a sense of validation, confirming the woman's place as object of desire. The man's force was a consequence of the women's attractiveness, and hence the ubiquity of coercion phantasies in female sexual life.

Although this may have a purchase in some cases, the facts of phantasy life tend to belie this as an overarching explanation. For starters, the man is rarely described as attractive, and more often he is depicted as hideous, repulsive, disgusting, anonymous or multiplied. Secondly, he is usually not overcome with passion, but may carry out sexual acts in a routine and businesslike manner, showing no emotional engagement at all, like a factory worker. The man's lack of interest may in itself have a sexual value, increasing the woman's arousal. In contrast to male coercion phantasies, in which the woman being aggressed may at a certain point become aroused, in many of the female scenarios this switch does not happen and the aggressor remains bored and disinterested.

How could these aspects of female phantasies be understood? One explanation given by early writers in the women's movement was that centuries of gender imparity, objectification, assault and lack of a space to articulate their own desires were bound to affect female subjectivity, so that phantasies were essentially either borrowed from men or constituted residues of their oppression. The conditions of oppression would become frameworks for arousal, and hence it would be a long and difficult process to reverse coercion phantasies into a more emancipated sexuality.

For some writers and activists, female sexuality was being identified too categorically here with victimization, with the result that anything which seemed to involve unequal power relations would be automatically stigmatized. This risked just telling women what they should and shouldn't be doing in bed, substituting one authoritative moral system for another. As Amber Hollibaugh put it in her celebrated dialogue with Cherrie Moraga, 'I don't want to live outside of power in my sexuality but I don't want to be trapped into a heterosexist concept of power either.' The fear of 'heterosexual control of phantasy' meant that there were no phantasies safe to have, and in her own sexual life the yielding of power in response to her lover's need could feel 'profoundly powerful and very unpassive'. And so phantasies of capture should be explored rather than excised as simply effects of what critics at the time called 'the prick in your head'.

Another perspective emphasized how we are always identified unconsciously with all the players in a phantasy scenario, and so the bored, disinterested men might actually represent a part of female subjectivity. If sex was experienced as a mechanical, emotionless duty by so many women, wasn't this being inverted in the coercion phantasy? Rather than an unengaged female figure, it is now the man or men who are just carrying out some dull factory-style task. The phantasy would thus be reversing the experiential side of gender roles of the typical marital-sex dynamics described by Kinsey and so many others. The only problem here is that coercion phantasies are equally common for women who report never having felt sex to be an emotionless duty imposed by men.

Were other factors also at play here, such as beliefs about how one's parents had sex? If one imagined one's mother as an asexual paragon of purity, for example, how could she have had sex unless she was forced? And this introduces what is perhaps the crucial feature of these phantasies: they treat the question of responsibility. To be forced into a situation of sexual submission overrides consent with coercion, and hence arguably allows the experience of sexual pleasure without guilt. As Carole Vance put it, 'Sex is always guilty before being proven innocent,' and it would follow that many sexual scenarios could be understood as attempts to demonstrate precisely this exoneration: 'Not guilty!'

In her compilation of female sexual phantasies, Nancy Friday noted the remarkable frequency of these verdicts, and how often phrases like 'I then had to . . .' or 'He made me . . .' would be used even if the scenario did not involve any obvious coercion. The person is not responsible for their enjoyment – especially enjoyment of a prohibited figure associated with the father – and all responsibility now sits squarely with the aggressor. If girls are socialized early to feel guilt at sexual pleasure, and that bodily arousal is somehow judged negatively and not permitted, these phantasies work by removing guilt and allowing the person to enjoy.

Similarly, the anonymity of the aggressors might signify a temporary escape both from the Oedipal aspect of the phantasy and from the feeling of being judged. Different aspects of sexual phantasy and practice can be recruited with this aim, from the wearing of masks to the casting of strangers to the adopting of positions which remove eye contact. Anonymity, as Friday points out, allows sex 'with no one to face: no known face, either, to account to afterwards'. Although we might like to think otherwise, sex is like a courtroom drama here, with different strategies for evading judgement and condemnation. Where men split, women anonymize.

As an analysand put it, speaking of her phantasy of being overpowered by a group of faceless men, 'I was being made to express a desire that I couldn't otherwise.' It was only the scenario of forceful submission that made her enjoyment possible, as agency was removed from her. Dyan Cannon described a similar process, but as well as shifting blame – 'I didn't want to be responsible for my actions' – she anaesthetized herself, cutting off her actual awareness of her body. 'I didn't feel a thing. I didn't want to feel the truth,' she wrote, and agency was situated unilaterally with her partner: 'I hated him, just hated him, for making me unfit to be any man's wife. I didn't want to be responsible for my actions so I made him responsible.'

The puzzling popularity with women of the film *Taken* becomes less bizarre when we recognize this question of responsibility. In this incredibly racist and misogynistic narrative, a father battles to rescue his daughter from sex traffickers, inflicting multiple homicides in the process. The idea of daddy's invincible love for his daughter perhaps distracts from the more unfortunate xenophobia of the film, but it is the scenario of abduction which provides the real fascination: to be 'taken' means all the responsibility is with the takers. The old and incorrect idea of female masochism surely covers over this question of the responsibility for pleasure: apparently masochistic scenarios are just a way of representing shifts of responsibility.

One might argue that there is actually a link here between the motif of abduction and that of the father's enduring love. In analysis, we witness at times a woman's ability to experience her body as sexual after a dream in which she is very literally a purely sexual object for her father. The dream may be horrifying and scary, but afterwards a different relation to the body may become possible. Would this represent a convergence of the themes of being taken and being chosen, with the consequent intertwining of removal of responsibility and the validation as a chosen, desirable object?

The idea of being chosen, however, may conceal another unconscious dimension, shaped by both personal and social history. When we explore female dreams of being an object for the father, the old motif of belonging emerges again and again: the daughter is the father's property. When Liam Neeson risks everything in his desperate quest to rescue his beloved child, isn't it ultimately in this sense of getting his property back? Women have for centuries been classified as male belongings, and hence the recompense for rape convictions were so often made to the woman's father and his family rather than to the victim herself. Sexual crime here was a property crime.

Even in the liberal 1960s, advocates and practitioners of the new sexual freedoms referred to 'wife trading' before it was sanitized into the more palatable 'swinging'. And if being a wife has historically so often presupposed bridal virginity – or at least its semblance – these notions of property have been deeply inscribed into the body itself. Many girls are socialized into the belief that the hymen is like the skin stretched over the barrel of a drum, which will then be broken during the first coitus, an image which is totally at odds with anatomical reality. Imagining the hymen as a seal perpetuates and reinforces the idea of male ownership, and of a woman's body as goods that can be intact or damaged.

Clinically, what we also see here so often is how a woman may experience both the powerful wish to belong to someone and the desire not to. In domestic abuse cases, friends and family may be baffled by the person's insistence on staying with the pathologically jealous and possessive husband, for example, even if their economic situation would allow them to leave and there seems to be some prospect of safety. Beyond the apparent conflict between basic notions of freedom and enslavement there is perhaps an Oedipal thread here: the image of belonging to the father may allow a child to separate from the mother, and so the feeling of 'belonging' and even of being property may come to acquire a special value and purpose.

Abduction dramas are extraordinarily popular today, and adults often find it nonsensical how these disturbing stories — usually in which a man kidnaps a girl or young woman — can be binge-watched by girls between eight and ten, before their attention turns to the more obvious teen shows depicting high-school romance. Movies like *Believe Me*, *Room*, *Abducted in Plain Sight* and *Girl in the Bunker* may fascinate through the brutal image of 'belonging' that they present, and, to a lesser extent, through the effects on the family who have lost their child.

When young analysands discuss these narratives, they focus on the bond between abductor and abductee, questioning what each might feel and sometimes imagining escape plans, and it is difficult not to sense here a tentative exploration of the question of what happens between a man and a girl sexually. What happens when a girl is 'chosen'? How can one both belong to someone and escape from them? Is force necessary to allow a physical contact that seems otherwise so dangerous and forbidden?

The emphasis on coercion here is reflected in female porn use. According to the available analytics, women are between 80 and 100 per cent more likely than men to browse the rubric 'rough sex', and submission scenarios have a high popularity. But it is worth noticing how porn searches for coercion are so often matched by those for female–female interactions, with the emphasis not on rough or brutalizing sex but on tender, gentler and slower sexual activity. Women who speak about this bifurcation don't see any contradiction at all between these two sets of scenarios, accessing the coercive or the tender according to their mood at the time. Significantly, where the submission narratives involve men objectifying a woman, the gentler porn does away with the man entirely, with sexual agency ascribed solely to female figures.

One might guess that submission scenarios would become more pervasive as girls are less likely to be taught that desire depends on love. If the early upbringing of girls in many societies since the 1920s taught them that they must love the person they have sex with and be romantically involved with them, this in a sense introduces a permission: love, as Claude Crépault observed, is the alibi of sexual desire. But as the connection between love and desire is weakened or undone in some parts of the contemporary world, it might suggest that other frameworks are required to absolve the person of responsibility.

Robert Stoller observed that the Masters and Johnson research, in which couples had sex in their lab, worked precisely because of the introduction of such a framework: it was the idea of the laboratory itself that legitimatized the sexual activity, relieving participants of the sense of guilt. And if female sexual activity has been more generally linked to some form of sacrifice – for love, for the man, for marriage, for children – as it gradually loses this dimension and sexual pleasure is affirmed as a value in itself, the problem is only made more acute. However objectionable and oppressive these notions of enforced altruism have been, the alternative leaves the question of responsibility open. If sexual enjoyment is an aim in itself, what price must be paid for it? How can responsibility for it be avoided or, in some sense, treated?

Erica Jong made the interesting observation here that in the days when sex and guilt were so openly fused, women who had the economic means would travel to Europe for hook-ups. This didn't just mean being far from home and the judgemental eyes of family and friends, but something much more specific: 'if you didn't speak the same language as the man you didn't have to feel guilty'. It was language here rather than, for example, a phantasy anonymization, that shifted responsibility, as if a shared language would bring with it a shared guilt. If both parties spoke the same language, speech would pin one down, accentuating one's position and accountability.

The recent TV show *The Language of Love* uses the same premiss, though shifts the accent from sexual desire to love. British and Spanish singletons meet at a country estate, and viewers can chart their burgeoning relationships. 'Is it possible to find love if you don't speak the same language?' asks the show's presenter, but despite positive reviews, the show was axed. We might wonder if a focus on sex would have made it more popular, with the strapline: 'Is it possible to have guilt-free sex if you don't speak the same language?'

*

We could distinguish here two different versions of this process of managing guilt. In the first, responsibility is shifted and the dimension of agency is passed over to the other side of the equation, as in submission scenarios. In the second, there is more of an emphasis on pain – which may or may not be part of submission phantasies – and can take many other forms, such as the desire to be spanked, punished or somehow mistreated. Pain here can be part of a licensing arrangement: it is the price to be paid for any subsequent pleasure. In both cases, however, pleasure cannot be a given as it is not permitted.

This surely explains the success of many of today's sex therapies, which work by granting permission. Analysts are often upset when after years of trying to help a patient overcome their sexual symptoms, a few sessions with a sex therapist produces brilliant results. It can't be a genuine cure, we complain, it must be a cure by suggestion, or somehow inauthentic. But it is a fact that these therapies can have real effects, and perhaps this is because what the therapist is essentially doing is telling the person that they have permission to have a sexed body. If they spent years growing up in an environment which effectively denied this, to have an authority figure override the original prohibitions on pleasure can have a powerful impact.

There is a curious inversion here of male sexual dynamics. Men often require a condition of prohibition in order to experience sexual arousal: the sexual 'object' must be forbidden or embody some form of inaccessibility. Hence the way in which some men feel compelled to pursue the wives of other men, as if the erotic charge really lies in the barrier, as the following gag shows. A man attending the funeral of a friend's wife, with whom he had been having an affair, sobs uncontrollably, until the husband says, 'Calm down, I'll be marrying again soon.' In contrast, many women can enjoy when they encounter less a prohibition than a permission: it's the opposite of Bluebeard's forbidden door, which is perhaps more of a male phantasy. Here, the arousal may be linked to the fact that the woman is, precisely, allowed to open the door.

When we have the opportunity to explore the forces that have blocked a girl from experiencing her body sexually, beyond the usual social mores we frequently find a deeper and unconscious interdiction: the fear of trespassing the space occupied by the mother. As Paula Webster put it, 'we may feel we betray her when we want more than she had', and, indeed, what she did or does have. If all sexual territory is felt to be occupied by her, the daughter may find it difficult to access her own space, and the punishment for doing so that appears in dreams and folklore is the sewing-up of the vulva. If a third party, then, can override the imagined authority of the mother, a sexual body can become possible.

This would also explain the clinical fact that a woman can sometimes access her own body as sexual after having a dream where she is the sexual object of her father, as we saw earlier. Although the dream is usually experienced as a nightmare, it may be the signature of a psychical process whereby the dreamer has found a way of avoiding the maternal trespass. If the phantasy image of the father is heavily sexualized, and he is represented as violent and coercive, he may be functioning to override the authority of the mother, wrenching the daughter away from her. What matters is to display a force that is stronger than that of the mother.

If coercion phantasies provide their own solution here, by absolving the daughter of responsibility for her bodily enjoyment, other scenarios that involve more apparent agency can have a similar function. Imagining herself as an erotic dancer or prostitute can be a condition of arousal for many women, and this is typically seen as an example of an interest in the Other woman, the one who is supposed to know something about sexuality, and who thus forms a pole of gravitation. She can be so fascinating because she embodies the mysterious object that men desire, the enigmatic question of femininity, etc. But at another level isn't the imaginary scenario effective because it treats the question of responsibility: the erotic dancer or prostitute has a symbolic and social role, and it is exactly this role that removes responsibility from her. It's her job. And so, like the coercion scenario, it distances responsibility for pleasure.

This perhaps illuminates the ubiquitous motif more generally of imagining being someone else during sex. The standard interpretation is to read this as a questioning of desire: if she is another person, what does the partner see in her? What arouses them? What is she for the other? But to be someone else might also mean, very simply, that one is absolved of responsibility for enjoyment. Abandoning oneself, one has a greater freedom, more right to a sexual body, and this may be why these phantasies are so frequent in female sexual life, and also why, perhaps, there may be an appeal to pornography. As a voice inside her said, 'Bad girl. Mustn't touch,' Sallie Tisdale reached out to porn not to learn more about sex but about crossing boundaries: 'I needed permission. I needed blessing.'

A further differentiation is helpful here. So, there is the idea of a permission that comes from a point beyond the mother, legitimizing the apparent trespass. Then there is the abdication of responsibility in the coercion phantasy, to avoid the shame of desire, or the use of pain as a licence for pleasure. But what we also find so often is a twist of the coercion scenario, in which it is less a question of others imposing their will on the person than of her not having to ask for whatever it is she might want. This was noticed by Karen Horney: the phantasy of an ideal partner who would reply before anything had been asked, with the crucial feature of making the asking – and hence the responsibility for desire – unnecessary. They had been second-guessed.

A woman explained her anger and disappointment at her partner when he gave her the very necklace she had chosen herself and valued greatly. Why hadn't he guessed beforehand? Why hadn't he anticipated what she had wanted? And crucially, why had she had to ask? There is a real erotic value in the bypassing of speech here, with its transactional circuits: so, the necklace should not have been part of a circuit of exchange but just given without ever having been asked for. When women sometimes evoke the 'expertise' of a phantasy lover, what makes them an expert is exactly this *knowing what to do* – without being told.

The success of Nancy Meyers' 2000 romcom, *What Women Want*, revolved around this premiss. An unpleasant and chauvinistic advertising executive played by Mel Gibson suddenly acquires the ability to read women's thoughts after being electrocuted, and uses this to his personal and professional advantage. The title of the movie is of course a statement rather than a question, and it refers ultimately neither to the executive himself nor to the particular content of a female character's thoughts but to the faculty of second-guessing, of knowing, as it were, in advance so that asking would never be required. 'What women want' on this model is just that someone else knows what they want, or, more precisely perhaps, that they don't have to ask.

It is instructive to imagine what a remake of this film would look like today. Viewers might have imagined that Mel Gibson was himself the referent of the title *What Women Want*, although since the allegations that he is a racist violent misogynist, the film might have to end after the electrocution scene. One might guess that an actor like Timothée Chalamet would have better prospects, as he embodies a gender fluidity that has traditionally been proscribed for mainstream male leads. And indeed, the film that is considered his career breakthrough – *Call Me By Your Name* – revolves around precisely this question of speaking and asking, and its link to sexuality. Come to think of it, maybe *Call Me By Your Name* was actually a remake of *What Women Want*.

To take another example, a woman described

her intense arousal when a partner would stroke her hair. 'It's always fire, it goes right through me, right inside me,' she explained. There was no difficulty for her in tracing this to the moments of intimacy in her childhood when her mother would stroke her hair affectionately. But if a clear line could be traced between the early and later experiences, it was exactly this guaranteed arousal that she had always felt unable to ask for: the pleasure 'was there waiting' but the responsibility for it could not be assumed.

*

The question of responsibility takes us back to the child's earliest experiences of bodily excitation. Although an infant will surely not even know the meaning of the term 'sexual', the phenomena of arousal are ubiquitous: the physical radiation of heat, vasocongestion of genital tissue, lubrication, the pressure exerted by the bladder and rectum on the vaginal walls. The physical signs of orgasm have even been reported in infants of less than one year: although ejaculation is absent, rhythmic body movements, pelvic motion, muscle tension in the abdomen, hips and back followed by a sudden release with spasming and anal contractions have been documented from around five months, and in one case – perhaps fantastically – even with a four-week-old girl.

Now, these experiences confront the child with two massive questions: why the change in the body? And how can these tension states best be treated? When our bodies change, most notoriously at puberty, a whole range of social and familial processes are introduced to frame and give meaning to the experience. The puberty rites of many cultures make these external and highly symbolic moments. And in those societies where medicine has progressively taken the place of religion, doctors find themselves the address-ees of people's worried concerns about bodily changes. Throughout our lives, our bodies require the injection of meaning, provided by a privileged third party.

Things are no different for the infant and child, but the task of acquiring meaning is made much more difficult by the fact that bodily changes adults associate with sexuality tend to be passed over in silence or mislabelled, as we have seen, and cloaked in an atmosphere of negative judgement. Bodily changes such as the radiation of heat, engorgement and pulsation can be felt as profoundly external, imposed against the child's will, just as muscle tension that does not lead to movement can be felt as an alien force. Children can even wish to be divested of their sexual organs to escape these states of fear, agitation and bodily tension.

Female arousal often uses the language here of disequilibrium and threat. 'Sexual feelings gave me a terrifying loss of control. When I get excited sexually I am sometimes not sure where my body is,' one woman explained, and that she would need to wear tight clothing to 'hold me together'. At peaks of excitation, she would feel 'pushed to the ground, pushed off the world. All support was gone. I was somewhere where there is no foundation, no hold. The orgasm was not pleasant. It was fearful.' Arousal led to 'a patch of nowhere'. In another description, 'An orgasm feels like heaven in the heat of hell.' Selma

Fraiberg described the sensations of panic and terror here felt by girls, and how vaginal contractions could make a child 'scared to death'. As Herschberger put it, the sensations of sexual arousal can be experienced as a 'strange enemy'.

And this is where the question of responsibility becomes so important. If an adult has the power to take away a state of tension felt in the child's body – say, hunger or thirst – it won't take long for them to become identified as the *source* of this state. Similarly, if an infant wants to change position, due to some muscular or epidermal discomfort, the adult's delay or failure to respond makes them the cause of the discomfort. The parent's power to respond thus has the strange effect of making them the one responsible for the initial problem.

Early states of arousal can have exactly the same effects. As the body changes, there is an appeal to the parent, who is then identified as their source, although the structure of the reproach can quickly be applied more widely. An eight-year-old girl with a crush on a boy in her class described how she felt physically aroused when near him but 'I feel angry with him because he makes me feel this way.' Although the notorious mood shifts of adolescence – and the equally important nine-to-ten-year period – tend to be explained in terms of children's search for independence from their parents, this same dimension may be absolutely present: bodily states of arousal and tension generate an (unknowing) appeal to the parent, who is then (unknowingly) blamed for their failure to treat them. The child may oscillate between repetitive attempts to engage a parent, frustration with them, and endless visits to the fridge, with the only sure thing being the knowledge that the remedy lies *outside* themselves.

Judith Kestenberg studied the variety of tension states in children's bodies, and argued that there were significant differences between the sites of internal agitation and the points on the body's surface where they would be localized to. She thought that the obvious apertures of the body and the sensate foci on them – the clitoris, the anus, the penis – made them particularly susceptible to localize confusing and disturbing internal rhythms of arousal and tension. As we grow up, she claimed, we learn to confuse the apertures with the interior. The clitoris, for example, is useful due to its starting–stopping quality, and manipulating it as a focus can help to relieve other, more diffuse genital tensions, described by one child as 'a sort of scattering'.

Similarly, Kestenberg thought that when girls contract the perineal muscles and press their thighs together, rather than just identifying this as a pleasure-giving masturbatory activity, it might be functioning to localize and limit other, more nagging and potentially overwhelming sensations further inside the body. As Karin Stephen had observed many years previously, the only force strong enough to treat sexuality is sexuality itself. This oscillation might be echoed in the difference between those areas with an abundant supply of nerve endings – such as the clitoral bulb – and those dependent on sympathetic and parasympathetic innervations, and the mixed innervation of striate and non-striate muscles involved in orgasm.

This use of one kind of sexual excitation to

control and limit another one is at the heart of many kinds of sexual practice, and is perhaps linked to the sensation of 'finishedness' that women sometimes speak of here. We have seen how masturbation and sex may be broken off in order to avoid the dangers of orgasm, but when orgasms do actually occur, they may sometimes still seem 'unfinished'. As psychoanalyst Natalie Shainess put it, 'There is the sense of something having taken place which makes further stimulation unwelcome and unavailing, without the perception of orgasm itself.' Masturbation may also be experienced as a matter of great urgency, and the handling of the genitals may be impatient, as if something has to be shaken off. In some cases, there can be a rush to stimulate the clitoris directly precisely in order to avoid another, more diffuse and overwhelming kind of bodily arousal.

The spreading excitement that is so difficult to bear generates an appeal primarily to the mother to take it away, to treat it in some way, as she has already proven she can with hunger and thirst. Yet the very fact that the bodily phenomena are both acutely avoided and unrecognized by adults makes this almost impossible. And hence the many ways that children experiment with their bodies, in particular with the sensations of fullness and emptiness, using the stomach, the bowel and the bladder. Subtle efforts to explore and structure internal experience tend to occur at exactly the points where the parental response is lacking or absent, and may take the form of efforts to open and close bodily apertures.

How people deal with these experiences will vary a great deal, and it is worth noting that the strategy which works for one person may not work for another. A woman explained that for her the internal feelings during masturbatory genital manipulation were just so disturbing that she found it easier to have sex with other people. The intensity of the bodily arousal was so much less with her clumsy partners that she did not find it at all threatening. Yet others may describe an inverse process, where interaction with another person carries far greater risks than the controlled space of a masturbation.

These muting functions of sex and masturbation are complicated in those cases where a very strong emotion accompanies them. Should we interpret this as a defence or diversion, or recognize its legitimacy – or both? I've occasionally heard female analysands speak of their feeling of 'pure hatred' of their mother while masturbating, and other analysts have also noticed this. How strange, that there is an intense feeling of hate in the very place where we might expect some sort of phantasy narrative or image. Questioned about this, one woman explained, 'I just don't know why, but the hate and the excitement are there together, they're like the same thing at the same time.'

The Hunts found to their surprise in their survey of sexual behaviour that around a third of their interviewees would masturbate when they felt rejected in love, so that the manipulation of their genitals was experienced as 'a form of revenge'. Note that it's less a phantasy scenario that plays out vengeance than the actual act of masturbating, an observation that echoes the conclusions of the infant researchers who claimed – contrary to their expectations – that early masturbation correlated with independence, and the effort to separate from the mother. Might it contain this element of revenge, or could the hatred that sometimes surfaces here involve a reproach to the mother for failing to treat one's own bodily sensations? Or could it be perhaps the only way it feels possible to actually have the emotion of hatred?

Another example here would be the question of urination during sex, as it may represent both the fear of losing bodily control and the attempt to impose order, through the opening and closing that it is felt to involve. We should remember that the stakes of bodily excitation are very high, and can be experienced as total collapse, bursting, uncontrolled urination and losing of the self, as the language of orgasm shows: 'I felt that if I let it go further I would pop. Not pop only in bed but all over . . . I dug my nails in and stopped myself.' Children and teenagers who discover orgasm through masturbation will often stop doing it so as to avoid these risks of disintegration. Excitement that children do not know how to treat or deal with may be transferred to the urinary tract, to generate urinary symptoms, such as frequent peeing, withholding urine and then peeing it out all at once, or rituals of opening and closing the urethra.

The appeal generated by the earliest moments of these bodily tension and excitation states helps to create a special avatar of the mother in the unconscious. Psychoanalysis has tended to privilege the representation of the mother as not giving or as depriving the child (of the usual suspects: milk, a penis) or as taking away (same). But Kestenberg's observations suggest that there is a third figure of the mother here, less the mother who fails to give or who deprives but rather of the mother who, precisely, fails to take away. This is the mother who is unable to or who refuses to take away the states of sexual tension in the child's body.

*

The reproach here perhaps finds a certain response in sex itself. When adults fuck, the most common single description of the feeling afterwards is 'relief', a term also used for the act of making someone come. If sex is a complex clearing house, as we have seen, for so many terrors and anxieties, one result might be the removal of tension states that the adults caring for us at the dawn of our lives failed to do. Sex, in this sense, takes away as much as it gives, and it might explain the sense of gratitude sometimes felt towards the other person, however selfish their actual sexual behaviour has been. The sexual partner has helped to remove the bodily state of arousal and tension, and sex has temporarily blotted out a whole range of other concerns.

The relief people report here also suggests that a terrible, mortal danger has been narrowly avoided. Sex as an act seems so unbelievable to children, and this sense of disbelief stays with us unconsciously throughout our lives. To have actually done it and survived it, with all the risks of bodily damage that it carries, is just unthinkable, and the tears and laughter that sometimes follow sex may be the signature of this accomplishment. And it is worth remembering how, unlike many other signs of emotion, tears and laughter are most often signs of relief, of having averted some calamity.

The words used for centuries to describe sex almost always refer simultaneously to cheating or dodging – to screw, to ream, to diddle, to swyve, to fuck, to trick, to jape – as if the sex act allows us for a moment to avoid catastrophe or outwit some malign force. Damage to the body and punishment have been averted in the very situation where we would be most at risk. And the odd mix of feelings that so often follow the sense of relief is perhaps testimony to this.

Men may need to make their escape even more concrete, by literally escaping into sleep after sex or physically leaving. Legman made the nice observation here that although Casanova is often seen as a paradigm of male sexual prowess, he actually spends half the time recorded in his *Memoirs* travelling: that is, getting away from his last sexual encounter. Men may feel disgust at themselves or at the other person, often with the idea that they have made concessions, and hence the urgent search for the next partner, and the conscious hatred of the other tends to conceal a self-hate here. If they are constantly engaged in defensive sexuality, trying to create and maintain splits which are always so fragile, their escape plans may be more pervasive and hurtful to others. For women, sex perhaps has this defensive quality less often; yet, as we have seen, different kinds of splitting may be operating which have their own consequences.

In the favourite phantasy of one of Jack Morin's patients, she is speeding home, sees a police car, yet doesn't slow down. The handsome policeman stops her, and suggests that there is a way for her to avoid getting a ticket: no prizes for guessing what happens next. Describing what made the scenario so exciting for her, she tells Morin that she was manipulating rather than being manipulated, and that she felt control over the cop. But the most intense and exciting part of the whole thing was that she gets to drive away without a ticket: 'I have triumphed!'

In other words, she has managed to avoid punishment, outwitting the law and the power of its representative. Pleasure without a price. That must be relief indeed, to be able to get away with this. If sex is a way of treating rage, despair and the feeling of being overwhelmed, it permits a very temporary medication of states of tension and terror. Sex acts do this through either dominations (oral, anal, muscular and genital) or conciliations via the same organs and body parts. We have seen how the same person may be in both these positions – and more – during a sexual encounter, and the oscillation between them may in itself generate excitement. And at the same time, bodily sensations are treated by fusions, localizations and blockings: one feeling fuses with another, or is localized to a point of sensate focus like the clitoris or the penis, or is blocked by another and apparently different feeling.

It is important to remember that, despite all this, sex is never just one thing. The same actions can have totally different meanings for different people, or for the same person at different moments in their life. Sex for a sixteen-year-old at a high-school party is unlikely to be the same as sex for a married or single forty-year-old, or for a soldier with their platoon in an occupied territory or for a recently widowed seventy-year-old. But at the same time, it will perhaps always involve bodily and emotional imbalances of power, small or large acts of violence and inflictions of pressure, which, as we have seen, may be in part effects of our early childhoods.

Given this baggage, it is quite surprising that people manage to have sex at all, and the many sexual 'performance' problems that people report are presumably testimony to this. Shouldn't these problems be read in fact as legitimate responses to one's circumstances? Bernard Apfelbaum observed that the actual ability to perform sex should in some cases be seen as a disorder. If someone is depressed, or angry with their partner, or feeling attacked by them, or grieving, or worried about their relationship, wouldn't this suggest that they shouldn't be able to have sex? Yet the fact that many continue to, and perform to script, means that sex and performance have in a way become separated. Sex becomes the very symptom of an alienation from oneself.

In her groundbreaking study *The Dialectic of Sex*, Shulamith Firestone argued that the only hope for a liberated sexuality – which she perhaps didn't really believe was possible — was to out-source all reproductive motherhood either to both sexes or, preferably, to forms of entirely artificial reproduction. Her rich and varied work is often reduced to this single thesis, which is then ridi-culed, but, even if it isn't going to happen, you can see the point: by excising the dependency relations of childhood and the sacrificial freight of mothers, all the skewed power relations of the infant–caregiver bond could potentially be redrafted, and would no longer have to be redirected to sexual acts themselves. Sex would no longer have to be a series of hidden and not-so-hidden acts of vio-lence, revenge and reversal.

If in sex we are playing out, pursuing and avenging many aspects of the early relationship with our caregivers, there will always be an imbal-ance of power, because that's how we started our lives. We were helpless, unable to express our-selves, and at the mercy of larger and more powerful bodies. Yet in sex there is almost always the sense of reversing helplessness, as we are momentarily the cause of feelings and sensations in the other person and sometimes in ourselves.

That's why people may feel such an erotic charge, in Amber Hollibaugh's words, as they 'see expressions of need sweep across their lovers' faces'. We are finally able to cause things, to have brief agency in a world where we tend to have none. And there is often a very fine line here between trying to be a cause of what someone else feels and the effort to master and control them: so, in effect, a kind of violence.

Beyond its reproductive shadow, sex perhaps exists to eroticize these dimensions of inequality, domination, force and causality. It involves an exploration and second-by-second elaboration of power relations, with rapid shifts in inequalities, as each person does something or refrains from doing something with their partner. These dynamics both contain social scripts and are shaped by them, dictating what can and cannot be done, and with whom. As Hollibaugh writes, 'Power is the heart, not just the beast, of all sexual inquiry.' When we say that phantasies have been ingrained in us through culture and socialization, and hence must be challenged, this is of course true, but what else could take their place if their very function is to do something with pain, trauma and oppression? If that is just what sex is, what else could it be?

Sex might be a way of turning our misery and oppression into a temporary and complex source of pleasure. An analysand who had grown up in Spain and had various sexual relationships there as a young man was shocked when, arriving in London, he found that the millennial women he slept with would often spit at his penis. Interpreting this as a cultural rather than a personal gesture – it was apparently not for purposes of lubrication – he made the decision not to protest, despite the fact that it made him uncomfortable: 'How could I say Stop, since women have had to endure men's oppression and tyranny for centuries?'

What is so interesting in his reaction was that sex was being understood as both a private and a public space, a space where it was possible to express anger at one's condition, yet in ways that are socialized to bring pleasure – occasionally. The problem, of course, is that the different parties involved will have different agendas and different angers, however we choose to interpret them. Sex is about so much more than sex – about history, about socialization, about anxiety, about guilt, about revenge, about violence, about love. When we assume it's just about pleasure and satisfaction, we fail to see what we need to see in order to rethink what sex both is and might be.

Notes

p. 3　Freud's conception of sex was of course far wider than pen–vag intercourse: for recent psychoanalytic approaches to sexuality, see Alenka Zupančič, *What is Sex?* (Cambridge, Massachusetts: MIT Press, 2017); and Jamieson Webster, *Disorganisation and Sex* (Brussels: Dividend, 2022). Kenneth Burke, *Permanence and Change* (New York: New Republic, 1936). Reading Freud through Burke here was suggested by John Gagnon and William Simon in *Sexual Conduct* (Chicago: Aldine, 1973). Seven seconds, see Terri Fisher et al., 'Sex on the brain? An examination of frequency of sexual cognitions as functions of gender, erotophilia, and social desirability', *Journal of Sex Research*, 49 (2012), pp. 69–77.

p. 4　Porn use, see Shira Tarrant, *The Pornography Industry: What Everyone Needs to Know* (Oxford: Oxford University Press, 2016), pp. 66–7.

p. 5 Biologists, see Clellan Ford and Frank Beach, *Patterns of Sexual Behavior* (New York: Ace, 1951); and Paul Hoch and Joseph Zubin, *Psychosexual Development in Health and Disease* (New York: Grune and Stratton, 1949).

p. 6 Indissolubility of sex and meaning, see Andrea Dworkin, *Intercourse* (New York: Basic Books, 1987).

p. 8 Surveys, see Clellan Ford and Frank Beach, *Patterns of Sexual Behavior*, op. cit.; Donald Marshall and Robert Suggs (eds), *Human Sexual Behavior* (Indiana: Institute for Sex Research, 1971); Frank Beach (ed.), *Human Sexuality in Four Perspectives* (Baltimore: Johns Hopkins University Press, 1976); Ruth Munroe et al. (eds), *Handbook of Cross-Cultural Human Development* (New York: Garland, 1981); and Roger Goodland, *A Bibliography of Sex Rites and Customs* (London: Routledge, 1931).

p. 9 Alfred Kinsey et al., *Sexual Behavior in the Human Male* (Philadelphia: Saunders, 1948), *Sexual Behavior in the Human Female* (Philadelphia: Saunders, 1953); and William Masters and Virginia Johnson, *Human Sexual Response* (Boston: Little, Brown, 1966). On the 'scientific' approach, see Jill Wood et al., 'Women's sexual desire: a feminist critique', *Journal of Sex Research*, 43 (2006), pp. 236–44; Lucy Bland and Laura Doan (eds),

Sexology in Culture: Labelling Bodies and Desires (University of Chicago Press, 1998); and Vern Bullough, *Science in the Bedroom: A History of Sex Research* (New York: Basic Books, 1994).

p. 10   Violence, see Lori Heise, 'Violence against women: the missing agenda', in Marge Koblinsky et al. (eds), *The Health of Women* (London: Routledge, 2019), pp. 171–96; Rachel Thompson, *Rough* (London: Square Peg, 2021); and William O'Donohue and Paul Schewe (eds), *Handbook of Sexual Assault and Sexual Assault Prevention* (Cham: Springer, 2019).

p. 11   Sigmund Freud, 'On the sexual theories of children' (1908), in *The Standard Edition of the Complete Psychological Works of Sigmund Freud*, vol. 9 (London: Hogarth, 1959), pp. 209–26.

p. 12   Anne Bernstein, *The Flight of the Stork*, 2nd ed. (Indianapolis: Perspectives Press, 1994). At twelve, see James Moore and Diane Kendall, 'Children's concepts of reproduction', *Journal of Sex Research*, 7 (1971), pp. 42–61. Inside of body, see Daniel Simons and Frank Keil, 'An abstract to concrete shift in the development of biological thought: the insides story', *Cognition*, 56 (1995), pp. 129–63; Warren Gadpaille, *The Cycles of Sex* (New York: Scribner's, 1975); and Ronald and Juliette Goldman, *Children's Sexual Thinking* (London: Routledge,

1982). Baby already inside, see B. Cohen and S. Parker, 'Sex information among nursery-school children', in Evelyn and Jerome Oremland (eds), *The Sexual and Gender Development of Young Children: The Role of the Educator* (Cambridge: Ballinger, 1977), pp. 181–90.

p. 13 Cut in belly, see Hans Kreitler and Shulamith Kreitler, 'Children's concepts of sexuality and birth', *Child Development*, 37 (1966), pp. 363–78. Belly buttons, see Eleanor Galenson and Herman Roiphe, *Infantile Origins of Sexual Identity* (New York: IUP, 1981).

p. 15 W. H. Trethowan and M. F. Conlon, 'The couvade syndrome', *British Journal of Psychiatry*, 111 (1965), pp. 57–66; Robert and Ruth Munroe, 'Male pregnancy symptoms and cross-sex identity in three societies', *Journal of Social Psychology*, 84 (1971), pp. 11–25. Smaller body, see J. M. Fawcett, 'The relationship between identification and patterns of change in spouse's body image during and after pregnancy', *International Journal of Nursing Studies*, 14 (1977), pp. 199–213.

p. 16 Ephron, see Karl and Anne Taylor Fleming, *The First Time* (New York: Simon and Schuster, 1975), pp. 80–86.

p. 17 'Easier to talk', cited in Harriet Lerner, 'Parental mislabeling of female genitals as a determinant of

penis envy and learning inhibitions in women',
Journal of the American Psychoanalytic Association,
24 (1976), pp. 269–83.

p. 19   Anus as pathway, see Seymour Fisher, *Sexual
Images of the Self: The Psychology of Erotic Sensa-
tions and Illusions* (Hillsdale, New Jersey: Lawrence
Erlbaum, 1989); and Heinz-Eugen Schramm's
monograph on the anus, *L.m.i.A.* (Tübingen:
Schlichtenmayer, 1960).

p. 20   Buttocks, pointed out by Gershon Legman,
Rationale of the Dirty Joke, vol. 2 (New York:
Breaking Point, 1975), p. 260. On Legman, see the
biography by Susan Davis, *Dirty Jokes and Bawdy
Songs: The Uncensored Life of Gershon Legman*
(Champaign, Illinois: University of Illinois Press,
2019). Asked in one study, 'Where is your body?',
43 per cent of kids pointed to their bottom, see
Carl Nils Johnson and Kimberly Kendrick, 'Body
partonomy: how children partition the human
body', *Developmental Psychology*, 20 (1984),
pp. 967–74.

p. 21   Sigmund Freud, 'On the sexual theories of
children', op. cit., p. 218; and Gershon Legman,
Rationale of the Dirty Joke, vol. 1 (New York: Grove
Press, 1968), pp. 256–318. Amber Hollibaugh, *My
Dangerous Desires: A Queer Girl Dreaming Her
Way Home* (Durham: Duke University Press,

2000), p. 85. See also Sharon Thompson, ' "Putting a big thing into a little hole ": teenage girls' accounts of sexual initiation', *Journal of Sex Research*, 27 (1990), pp. 341–61.

p. 22 Andrea Dworkin, 'Why so-called radical men love and need pornography', in Laura Lederer (ed.), *Take Back the Night: Women on Pornography* (New York: Morrow, 1980), p. 152. Freud's students, see Gregory Zilboorg, 'Masculine and feminine', *Psychiatry*, 7 (1941), pp. 257–96; Karen Horney, 'The denial of the vagina', *International Journal of Psychoanalysis*, 14 (1933), pp. 57–70; and Ernest Jones, 'Early development of female sexuality', *International Journal of Psychoanalysis*, 8 (1927), pp. 459–72.

p. 25 Selma Fraiberg, 'Tales of the discovery of the secret treasure', *Psychoanalytic Study of the Child*, 9 (1954), pp. 218–41.

p. 26 Template, see Judith Kestenberg, *Children and Parents: Psychoanalytic Studies of Development* (New York: Aronson, 1975), pp. 89, 142.

p. 27 Claude Crépault, *Les Fantasmes: l'érotisme et la sexualité* (Paris: Odile Jacob, 2007), p. 24.

p. 29 Kate Webb, see Susan Brownmiller, *Against Our Will: Men, Women and Rape* (New York: Bantam, 1975), p. 44. Sex and the media, see Roxane Gay, 'The careless language of sexual violence', in

Bad Feminist (New York: HarperCollins, 2014), pp. 128–36.

p. 30 Drivers, see Gershon Legman, *Rationale of the Dirty Joke*, vol. 2, op. cit., p. 720. Sigmund Freud, *The Psychopathology of Everyday Life* (1901), in *The Standard Edition of the Complete Psychological Works of Sigmund Freud*, vol. 6 (London: Hogarth, 1960), footnote p. 181. On what gets missed in wave divisions, see the important study by Shira Tarrant, *When Sex Became Gender* (New York: Routledge, 2006).

p. 31 Ruth Herschberger, *Adam's Rib* (New York: Pellegrini and Cudahy, 1948). On Herschberger, see Shira Tarrant, *When Sex Became Gender*, op. cit.

p. 33 On gendered socialization, the early studies are sadly still topical today: Viola Klein, *The Feminine Character* (London: Routledge, 1946); B. M. Spinley, *The Deprived and the Privileged* (London: Routledge, 1953); Lois Barclay Murphy, *The Widening World of Childhood* (New York: Basic Books, 1962); Judith Bardwick (ed.), *Readings on the Psychology of Women* (New York: Harper Row, 1972); Shirley Angrist, 'The study of sex roles', *Journal of Social Issues*, 25 (1969), pp. 215–32; Eleanor Maccoby and Carol Jacklin, *The Psychology of Sex Differences* (Stanford University Press, 1974);

and Lucile Duberman (ed.), *Gender and Sex in Society* (New York: Praeger, 1975).

p. 35 Shulamith Firestone, *The Dialectic of Sex* (New York: Morrow, 1970), p.51.

p. 37 Joan Nestle, 'The fem question', in Carole Vance (ed.), *Pleasure and Danger* (New York: Routledge, 1984), pp. 232–41. Skewer: this story is already in the Bible, Numbers 25:6–15, where the copulating Zimri and Cozbi are speared by the priest Phinehas. Edge, see Seymour Fisher, *Development and Structure of the Body Image*, 2 vols (Hillsdale, New Jersey: Lawrence Erlbaum, 1986).

p. 38 Exudations, see Edmund Leach, 'Anthropological aspects of language: animal categories and verbal abuse', in Eric Lenneberg (ed.), *New Directions in the Study of Language* (Cambridge, Massachusetts: MIT Press, 1964), pp. 23–63.

p. 39 Weapon and trap, see Wolfgang Lederer, *The Fear of Women* (New York: Harcourt, 1968); and Susan Brownmiller, *Against Our Will: Men, Women and Rape*, op. cit.

p. 41 Mislabelling, see James Moore and Diane Kendall, 'Children's concepts of reproduction', op. cit.; Seymour Fisher, *Development and Structure of the Body Image*, op. cit.; and John Gagnon and William Simon, *Sexual Conduct*, op. cit. Body image, see Seymour Fisher, *Development and Structure of the Body Image*, vol. 2, op. cit., p. 632. YouGov survey (2019): https://yougov.co.uk/topics/health/articles-reports/2019/03/08/half-brits-dont-know-where-vagina-and-its-not-just

p. 42　Prostate, see Judith Kestenberg, 'Dr Judith S. Kestenberg talks to Kristina Stanton', *Free Associations*, 2 (1991), pp. 157–74.

p. 43　G. G. Giles et al., 'Sexual factors and prostate cancer', *British Journal of Urology International*, 92 (2003), pp. 211–16; P. Dimitropoulou et al., 'Sexual activity and prostate cancer risk in men diagnosed at a younger age', *British Journal of Urology International*, 103 (2009), pp. 178–85; and M. F. Leitzmann et al., 'Ejaculation frequency and subsequent risk of prostate cancer', *Journal of the American Medical Association*, 291 (2004), pp. 1578–86.

p. 44　Twenty-five per cent, see https://www.jostrust.org.uk/node/1073042; and Vanessa Schick, 'Examining the vulva: the relationship between female genital aesthetic perception and gynecological care', dissertation, University of Massachusetts Amherst (2010).

p. 45　Sexual enlightenment, see Gershon Legman, *Rationale of the Dirty Joke*, vol. 1, op. cit., p. 50.

p. 46   Kids' comics, see Gershon Legman, *Love and Death* (New York: Hacker, 1963). Margaret Atwood, *Murder in the Dark* (London: Jonathan Cape, 1984), pp. 47–50.

p. 47   Not me, see N. Blackman, 'Pleasure and touching: their significance in the development of the pre-school child', in J. M. Samson (ed.), *Proceedings of the International Symposium on Childhood and Sexuality* (Montreal: Vivantes, 1980), pp. 112–24. Talking genitals, see Garin, 'Le chevalier qui faisait parler les cons et les culs', in *Nocrion, contre Allobroge* (Brussels: Gay et Douce, 1881); and Emma Rees, *The Vagina: A Literary and Cultural History* (New York: Bloomsbury, 2013).

p. 50   John Gagnon and William Simon, *Sexual Conduct*, op. cit., p. 262. Intensity, ibid., p. 56. Early studies, see H. M. Halverson, 'Genital and sphincter behavior of the male infant', *Pedagogical Seminary and Journal of Genetic Psychology*, 56 (1940), pp. 95–136; and Glenn Ramsey, 'The sexual development of boys', *American Journal of Psychology*, 56 (1943), pp. 217–33.

p. 51   Lubrication from many sources, see Floyd Martinson, 'Erotism in infancy and childhood', *Journal of Sex Research*, 12 (1976), pp. 251–62; and John Gagnon, *Human Sexualities* (Illinois: Scott, Foresman Co., 1977), p. 135. Accident, see Claude

Crépault, *Les Fantasmes: l'érotisme et la sexualité*, op. cit., p. 28.

p. 52   Roxane Gay, *Hunger* (New York: HarperCollins, 2017), p. 266.

p. 53   Clergyman, see Laud Humphreys, *Tearoom Trade: Impersonal Sex in Public Places* (Chicago: Aldine, 1970).

p. 54   Changing views on arousal, see Dolf Zillmann, *Connections Between Sexuality and Aggression*, 2nd ed. (New Jersey: Erlbaum, 1998), p. 195; G. Norton and D. Jehu, 'The role of anxiety in sexual dysfunction: a review', *Archives of Sexual Behavior*, 2 (1984), pp. 165–83; D. G. Dutton and A. P. Aron, 'Some evidence for heightened sexual attraction under conditions of high anxiety', *Journal of Personality and Social Psychology*, 30 (1974), pp. 510–11; David Barlow, 'The role of anxiety on sexual arousal', *Archives of Sexual Behavior*, 19 (1990), pp. 569–81; David Barlow, 'Causes of sexual dysfunction: the role of anxiety and cognitive interference', *Journal of Consulting and Clinical Psychology*, 54 (1986), pp. 140–48; and Valerie Hale and Donald Strassberg, 'The role of anxiety on sexual arousal', *Archives of Sexual Behavior*, 19 (1990), pp. 569–80. Magnus Hirschfeld, *The Sexual History of the World War* (New York: Cadillac, 1941),

p. 76. Knives, see Philip Sarrel and William Masters, 'Sexual molestation of men by women', *Archives of Sexual Behavior*, 11 (1982), pp. 117–31; David Barlow et al., 'Anxiety increases sexual arousal', *Journal of Abnormal Psychology*, 92 (1983), pp. 49–54; and David Barlow, 'Causes of sexual dysfunction: the role of anxiety and cognitive interference', *Journal of Consulting and Clinical Psychology*, 54 (1986), pp. 140–48.

p. 55 Forgetting, see Eleanor Galenson and Herman Roiphe, *Infantile Origins of Sexual Identity*, op. cit., p. 250.

p. 57 On global use of Pornhub in early pandemic: https://www.pornhub.com/insights/coronavirus; and Fabio Zattoni et al., 'The impact of COVID-19 pandemic on pornography habits: a global analysis of Google Trends', *Sexual Medicine Journal*, 33 (2021), pp. 824–31.

p. 58 Judged versus actual arousal, see Seymour Fisher, *Sexual Images of the Self*, op. cit.; Seymour Fisher, *Development and Structure of the Body Image*, op. cit., vol. 1, pp. 27–32; and D. W. Briddell et al., 'Effects of alcohol and cognitive set on sexual arousal to deviant stimuli', *Journal of Abnormal Psychology*, 87 (1978), pp. 418–30. Men more aroused by images of women in pain than pleasure, see A. B. Heilbrun and D. T. Seif, 'Erotic value of

female distress in sexually explicit photographs',
Journal of Sex Research, 24 (1988), pp. 47–57. Alcohol study, see D. W. Briddell et al., 'Effects of
alcohol and cognitive set on sexual arousal to
deviant stimuli', op. cit.

p. 59   Difference between orgasm and ejaculation, see
Mina Robbins and Gordon Jensen, 'Multiple
orgasm in males', in Robert Gemme and Connie
Christine Wheeler, *Progress in Sexology* (New
York: Plenum, 1977), pp. 323–8; Alfred Kinsey
et al., *Sexual Behavior in the Human Male*, op.
cit., pp. 179–80; and Marian Dunn and J. E.
Trost, 'Male multiple orgasms: a descriptive
study', *Archives of Sexual Behavior*, 18 (1989), pp.
377–87. Lawrence, see Seymour Fisher, *The
Female Orgasm* (New York: Basic Books, 1973),
p. 382.

p. 61   Father moving away, see Warren Gadpaille, *The
Cycles of Sex*, op. cit., pp. 170–71, 297.

p. 64   Jack Morin, *The Erotic Mind* (New York: Harper
Perennial, 1996), p. 197.

p. 65   2016, see Martin Seehuus et al., 'On the content of
"real world" sexual fantasy: results from an analysis of 250,000+ anonymous text-based erotic
fantasies', *Archives of Sexual Behavior*, 48 (2019),
pp. 725–37. DIY porn, see Shira Tarrant, *The
Pornography Industry*, op. cit., p. 91.

p. 66   John Gagnon and William Simon, *Sexual Conduct*, op. cit., p. 263.

p. 68   Robert Stoller, *Sexual Excitement* (New York: Routledge, 1979), pp. 6–7; Marta Meana, 'Elucidating women's (hetero)sexual desire: definitional challenges and content expansion', *Journal of Sex Research*, 47 (2010), pp. 104–22; Marie Darrieussecq, *A Brief Stay With the Living* (London: Faber and Faber, 2003), pp. 93–5; and Anna Clark, *Desire: A History of European Sexuality*, 2nd ed. (London: Routledge, 2019).

p. 69   Scripts, see John Gagnon and William Simon, *Sexual Conduct*, op. cit.; and John Gagnon, *An Interpretation of Desire* (Chicago: University of Chicago Press, 2004).

p. 71   Clellan Ford and Frank Beach, *Patterns of Sexual Behavior*, op. cit.; Donald Marshall and Robert Suggs (eds), *Human Sexual Behavior*, op. cit.; Frank Beach (ed.), *Human Sexuality in Four Perspectives*, op. cit.; and Caroline Brettell and Carolyn Sargent, *Gender in Cross-cultural Perspective* (New York: Routledge, 2016).

p. 72   Nipples, see John Gagnon, *Human Sexualities*, op. cit., p. 129. Choking, see R. W. Byard and N. H. Bramwell, 'Autoerotic death in females: an underdiagnosed syndrome?', *American Journal of Forensic Medical Pathology*, 9 (1988), pp. 252–4;

Claude Crépault, *Les Fantasmes: l'érotisme et la sexualité*, op. cit., p. 28; Helene Deutsch, *The Psychology of Women*, vol. 1 (New York: Grune and Stratton, 1944), pp. 176, 344; R. E. Litman and C. Swearingen, 'Bondage and suicide', *Archives of General Psychiatry*, 27 (1972), pp. 80–85; Anny Sauvageau and Stéphanie Racette, 'Autoerotic deaths in the literature from 1954 to 2004: a review', *Journal of Forensic Science*, 51 (2006), pp. 140–46; and Park Dietz, 'Recurrent discovery of autoerotic asphyxia', in Robert Hazewood et al. (eds), *Autoerotic Fatalities* (Lexington: D. C. Heath, 1983), pp. 13–44.

p. 73   Clapping, see *The School of Venus or the Ladies Delight* (London: 1680); Thomas Nashe, *Choise of Valentines or the Merie Ballad of Nashe His Dildo* (1592–3), ed. John Farmer (London: 1899). Social class, see Alfred Kinsey et al., *Sexual Behavior in the Human Male*, op. cit.; and Seymour Fisher, *The Female Orgasm*, op. cit. Jenny Higgins and Irene Browne, 'Sexual needs, control, and refusal: how "doing" class and gender influences sexual risk-taking', *Journal of Sexual Research*, 45 (2008), pp. 233–45.

p. 74   L. Van der Weck-Erlen, *Das goldene Buch der Liebe* (Vienna: Stern, 1907), vol. 2; and Sigmund Freud, 'The Uncanny' (1919), in *The Standard*

Edition of the Complete Psychological Works of Sigmund Freud, vol. 17 (London: Hogarth, 1955), pp. 219–56. Trains, see Donald Levine (ed.), *Simmel: Individuality and Social Forms* (Chicago: University of Chicago Press, 1971); and Iwan Bloch, *Die Prostitution*, vol. 2 (Berlin: Marcus, 1925).

p. 80   Margaret Mead, *Male and Female* (New York: Morrow, 1949), p. 266.

p. 87   Class barriers, see Murray Davis, *Smut* (Chicago: University of Chicago Press, 1983), p. 19. On the milieu, see Joseph Slade, 'Pornographic theaters off Times Square', in Ray Rist (ed.), *The Pornography Controversy* (New Jersey: Transaction, 1975), pp. 119–39.

p. 89   Orgasm, see Seymour Fisher, *The Female Orgasm*, op. cit.; Robert Muchembled, *Orgasm and the West: A History of Pleasure from the Sixteenth Century to the Present* (Cambridge: Polity, 2008); and Gérard Pommier, *What Does It Mean to 'Make Love'?* (London: Routledge, 2023).

p. 90   William Masters and Virginia Johnson, *Human Sexual Response*, op. cit., pp. 56–67. On Masters and Johnson's linear model, see Rosemary Basson, 'Women's sexual desire – disordered or misunderstood?', *Journal of Sex and Marital Therapy*, 28 (2002), pp. 17–28. Emily Opperman et al., '"It feels so good it almost hurts": young adults' experience of orgasm and sexual pleasure', *Journal of Sex Research*, 51 (2014), pp. 503–15.

p. 91 Celia Roberts et al., 'Faking it: the story of "Ohh!"', *Women's Studies International Forum*, 18 (1995), pp. 523–32; and C. L. Muehlenhard and S. K. Shippee, 'Men and women's reports of pretending orgasm', *Journal of Sex Research*, 47 (2010), pp. 552–67. Marie Darrieussecq, *Simulatrix* (Paris: Les Inrockuptibles, 2003). Faking was seen for centuries as a basic part of woman's engagement in sex, see Ferrante Pallavicino, *The Whore's Rhetorik* (1683) (New York: Astor-Honor, 1961).

p. 92 Bernard Apfelbaum, 'Sexual reality and how we dismiss it': https://egoanalysisessays.wordpress.com/2016/09/26/sexual-reality-and-how-we-dismiss-it/

p. 93 Morton Hunt, *Sexual Behavior in the 1970s* (Chicago: Playboy, 1974), p. 160.

p. 94 Marjorie Brierley, 'Specific determinants in feminine development', *International Journal of Psychoanalysis*, 17 (1936), pp. 163–80. Sigmund Freud, 'On the sexual theories of children', op. cit., p. 216.

p. 95 William Masters and Virginia Johnson, *Human Sexual Response*, op. cit. See the commentary in Paul Robinson, *The Modernization of Sex* (New York: Harper and Row, 1976). Mary Jane Sherfey,

The Nature and Evolution of Female Sexuality (New York: Random House, 1966); and Inge and Sten Hegeler, *ABZ of Love* (New York: Medical Press, 1963). Shere Hite, *The Hite Report* (New York: Macmillan, 1976).

p. 96 Philippe Charlier et al., 'A brief history of the clitoris', *Archives of Sexual Behavior*, 49 (2020), pp. 47–8. Note how many of the ideas about the clitoris attributed to Masters and Johnson had been elaborated much earlier: Félix Roubaud, *Traite de l'impuissance et de la sterilité chez l'homme et chez la femme* (Paris: Bailliere, 1855); and Heinrich Kisch, *The Sexual Life of Woman in its Physiological, Pathological and Hygienic Aspects* (New York: Rebman, 1910). Spinal, see Dolf Zillmann, *Connections Between Sexuality and Aggression*, op. cit., p. 103; Beverly Whipple et al., 'Physiological correlates of imagery-induced orgasm in women', *Archives of Sexual Behavior*, 21 (1992), pp. 121–33; and R. J. Lewin and G. Wagner, 'Self-reported central sexual arousal without vaginal arousal – duplicity or veracity revealed by objective measurement', *Journal of Sex Research*, 23 (1987), pp. 540–44. Two to four seconds, see Zella Luria and Mitchel Rose, *Psychology of Human Sexuality* (Chichester: Wiley, 1979), p. 178.

p. 97 Carol Queen, *Real Live Nude Girl* (San Francisco: Cleis, 1997), p. 91. Just watching porn, see Seymour Fisher, *Sexual Images of the Self*, op. cit., p. 64.

p. 98 Forty per cent and critique of Masters and Johnson, see Carol Butler, 'New data about female sexual response', *Journal of Sex and Marital Therapy*, 2 (1976), pp. 40–46; Mary Jo Sholty et al., 'Female orgasmic experience: a subjective study', *Archives of Sexual Behavior*, 13 (1984), pp. 155–64; and P. M. Bentler and W. H. Peeler, 'Models of female orgasm', *Archives of Sexual Behavior*, 8 (1979), pp. 405–23. Selma Fraiberg, 'Some characteristics of genital arousal and discharge in latency girls', *Psychoanalytic Study of the Child*, 27 (1972), pp. 439–75. Dead feeling, see Seymour Fisher, *The Female Orgasm*, op. cit., pp. 300, 311–13. Ruth Herschberger, *Adam's Rib*, op. cit., p. 124.

p. 99 Twenty-five per cent, see Gerda de Bruijn, 'From masturbation to orgasms with a partner: how some women bridge the gap – and why others don't', *Journal of Sex and Marital Therapy*, 8 (1982), pp. 151–67. Male orgasm as end of sexual encounter in 94.7 per cent of porn, see K. McPhillips et al., 'Defining (hetero)sex: how imperative is the "coital imperative"?', *Women's Studies International Forum*, 24 (2001), pp. 229–40.

p. 100 Josephine and Irving Singer, 'Types of female orgasm', *Journal of Sex Research*, 8 (1972), pp. 255–67.

p. 102 Doris Lessing, *The Golden Notebook* (New York: Simon and Schuster, 1962), p. 179. Crygasm, see Stephanie Theobald, *Sex Drive* (London: Unbound, 2017), p. 117.

p. 103 Edrita Fried, *The Ego in Love and Sexuality* (New York: Grune and Stratton, 1960), p. 41. Edith Jacobson, *Depression* (New York: IUP, 1971), p. 253.

p. 104 Anaïs Nin, *Delta of Venus* (London: Penguin, 2000), pp. 28–48. True to oneself, see Bernard Apfelbaum, 'Sexual reality and how we dismiss it', op. cit.

p. 107 Fabricating, see Friedrich Karl Forberg, *Manual of Classical Erotology* (Manchester: Julian Smithson, 1884), p. 34.

p. 108 Barber, see Abraham Freedman, 'Psychoanalytic study of an unusual perversion', *Journal of the American Psychoanalytic Association*, 26 (1978), pp. 749–77.

p. 110 Milgram, see Gershon Legman, *Rationale of the Dirty Joke*, vol. 2, op. cit., p. 8.

p. 113 Threats to body, see Seymour Fisher, *Development and Structure of the Body Image*, vol. 1, op. cit.; and E. Goodenough Pitcher and E. Prelinger,

Children Tell Stories: An Analysis of Fantasy (New York: IUP, 1963).

p. 114 Membership systems, see William Domhoff, *The Bohemian Grove and Other Retreats: A Study in Ruling Class Cohesiveness* (New York: Harper and Row, 1974). Boundaries, see Seymour Fisher, *Development and Structure of the Body Image*, vol. 1, op. cit., p. 102. Brides pregnant at marriage, see Barry Reay and Kim M. Phillips, *Sex Before Sexuality: A Premodern History* (Cambridge: Polity, 2011), p. 51.

p. 115 Gershon Legman, *Rationale of the Dirty Joke*, vol. 1, op. cit., p. 623.

p. 116 Selma Fraiberg, 'Enlightenment and confusion', *Psychoanalytic Study of the Child*, 6 (1951), pp. 325–35.

p. 118 Margaret Mead, *Male and Female*, op. cit., p. 116.

p. 121 Compare with the report in the *Boston Globe* on 14 March 1976, according to which 60 per cent of clients of high-level escorts are political figures seeking flagellation while held in bondage.

p. 124 Sterling North, 'A national disgrace', *Chicago Daily News*, 8 May 1940.

p. 125 Cutting male body, see R. L. Munroe et al., 'Male sex-role resolutions', in Ruth Munroe et al. (eds), *Handbook of Cross-Cultural Human Development*, op. cit., pp. 611–32.

p. 126 Clellan Ford and Frank Beach, *Patterns of Sexual Behavior*, op. cit., p. 263. Hustler work, see John Gagnon and William Simon, *Sexual Conduct*, op. cit., p. 264; Albert Reiss, 'The social integration of queers and peers', *Social Problems*, 9 (1961), pp. 102–20; and Laud Humphreys, *Tearoom Trade: Impersonal Sex in Public Places*, op. cit.

p. 128 Stephanie Theobald, *Sex Drive*, op. cit. Shere Hite, *The Hite Report*, op. cit., p. 141.

p. 129 Deirdre English, Amber Hollibaugh and Gayle Rubin, 'Talking sex: a conversation on sexuality and feminism', *Feminist Review*, 11 (1982), pp. 40–52. See also the recent discussion in Amia Srinivasan, *The Right to Sex* (London: Bloomsbury, 2021), pp. 73–122.

p. 130 Acts and identities, see Michel Foucault, *The History of Sexuality* (New York: Pantheon, 1978); Jonathan Katz, *The Invention of Heterosexuality* (New York: Penguin, 1995); David Halperin, 'Forgetting Foucault: acts, identity and the history of sexuality', in Kim M. Phillips and Barry Reay (eds), *Sexualities in History* (New York: Routledge, 2002), pp. 42–68; and Sarah Salih, 'Sexual identities: a medieval perspective', in Tom Betteridge (ed.), *Sodomy in Early Modern Europe* (Manchester: Manchester University Press, 2002), pp. 121–30. Contra ideas of early gender fluidity, note how desiring a woman could be given as a defence in sodomy trials, see Iwan Bloch, *Sexual Life in England, Past and Present* (London: Aldor, 1938), p. 334.

p. 131 *Kinaidos*, see Friedrich Karl Forberg, *Manual of Classical Erotology*, op. cit., p. 53; David Halperin, *How to Do the History of Male Homosexuality* (Chicago: University of Chicago Press, 2002); and John Winkler, *The Constraints of Desire* (New York: Routledge, 1990), pp. 45–70.

p. 132 Sodomy, see Vern Bullough, *Sexual Variance in Society and History* (New York: Wiley, 1976); and Mark Jordan, *The Invention of Sodomy in Christian Theology* (Chicago: University of Chicago Press, 1997).

p. 134 Categories, see John Gagnon and William Simon, *Sexual Conduct*, op. cit.; Khaled El-Rouayheb, *Before Homosexuality in the Arab-Islamic World 1500–1800* (Chicago: University of Chicago Press, 2005); Carrol Smith-Rosenberg, 'The female world of love and ritual: relations between women in nineteenth-century America', *Signs*, 9 (1985), pp. 1–29; Valerie Traub, *The Renaissance of Lesbianism in Early Modern England* (Cambridge: Cambridge University Press, 2002); Barry Reay and Kim M. Phillips, *Sex Before Sexuality*, op. cit.; Martha Vicinus, *Intimate Friends: Women Who Loved Women, 1778–1928* (Chicago: University of Chicago Press, 2004); and Alan Bray,

Homosexuality in Renaissance England (New York: Columbia University Press, 1995).

p. 135 Male–male penetration, see Gilbert Herdt (ed.), *Ritualized Homosexuality in Melanesia* (Berkeley, California: University of California Press, 1984); Bruce Knauft, *South Coast New Guinea Cultures* (Cambridge: Cambridge University Press, 1993); Gilbert Herdt, *The Sambia: Ritual, Sexuality, and Change in Papua New Guinea* (Belmont: Wadsworth, 2006); David Greenberg, *The Construction of Homosexuality* (Chicago: University of Chicago Press, 1988); and Bruce Knauft, 'Whatever happened to ritualised homosexuality? Modern sexual subjects in Melanesia and elsewhere', *Annual Review of Sex Research*, 14 (2003), pp. 137–59.

p. 139 Merle Miller, 'What it means to be a homosexual', *New York Times Magazine*, 17 January 1971. Consequences not causes, see Edrita Fried, *The Ego in Love and Sexuality*, op. cit., p. 102; and John Gagnon and William Simon, *Sexual Conduct*, op. cit., p. 135.

p. 140 Margaret Mead, *Male and Female*, op. cit.; and Clellan Ford and Frank Beach, *Patterns of Sexual Behavior*, op. cit., pp. 262–3. Sex practices, see John Gagnon and William Simon, *Sexual Conduct*, op. cit.; and Carol Queen and Lawrence

Schimel (eds), *PoMoSexuals: Challenging Assumptions About Gender and Sexuality* (San Francisco: Cleis, 1997).

p. 141 D. Travers Scott, 'Le freak, c'est chic! Le fag, quelle drag!', in Carol Queen and Lawrence Schimel (eds), *PoMoSexuals: Challenging Assumptions About Gender and Sexuality*, op. cit., pp. 62–8.

p. 143 Miquel Missé, *The Myth of the Wrong Body* (Cambridge: Polity, 2022); and Joanne Meyerowitz, *How Sex Changed: A History of Transsexuality in the United States* (Cambridge, Massachusetts: Harvard University Press, 2004).

p. 144 Ronald and Juliette Goldman, *Children's Sexual Thinking*, op. cit.; *Fortune* magazine (autumn 1946); and Margaret Mead, *Male and Female*, op. cit., p. 247. On separating, see Geneviève Morel, *The Law of the Mother* (London: Routledge, 2018).

p. 146 Lord Kennet, see Wayland Young, *Eros Denied*, op. cit. Phyllis and Eberhard Kronhausen came to the same conclusion re dildoes in *The Sexually Responsive Woman* (New York: Ballantine, 1965) and in *Erotic Fantasies: A Study of the Sexual Imagination* (New York: Grove Press, 1969), pp. 325–6. Anne Lister notes how she 'thought of her using phallus to her friend': see wyascatablogue. wordpress.com.

p. 147 Stories and rhymes, see Gershon Legman, *Rationale of the Dirty Joke*, vol. 2, op. cit., pp. 140–83. Butch-femme, see Joan Nestle, 'The fem question', in Carole Vance (ed.), *Pleasure and Danger*, op. cit., pp. 232–41.

p. 150 Stone phalli, see Magnus Hirschfeld, *The Sexual History of the World War*, op. cit., p. 82.

p. 151 Until wound heals, Donald Marshall and Robert Suggs (eds), *Human Sexual Behavior*, op. cit., p. 81.

p. 152 Raleigh, see John Aubrey, *Brief Lives*, edited by John Collier (London: Peter Davies, 1931), pp. 42–3.

p. 153 Reskinning, see Allen Edwardes, *Erotica Judaica* (New York: Julian Press, 1967).

p. 154 Bridge, see D. G. Dutton and A. P. Aron, 'Some evidence for heightened sexual attraction under conditions of high anxiety', op. cit.

p. 155 Fellatio, see Gershon Legman, *Oral Techniques in Sexual Intercourse* (New York: Julian, 1969); Martin Monto, 'Prostitution and fellatio', *Journal of Sex Research*, 38 (2001), pp. 140–45; Laud Humphreys, *Tearoom Trade*, op. cit., pp. 51–2; and Barry Eleano and Vern Bullough, *An Annotated Bibliography of Prostitution* (New York: Garland, 1976).

p. 159 Inversion of the violent thrusting, see Rochester's 1680 poem 'The Wish' where he imagines himself as a sperm in the womb: 'There steep'd in Lust, nine months I wou'd remain / Then boldy fuck my Passage out again.'

p. 160 On Rolling Stones, see Susan Brownmiller, *Against Our Will: Men, Women and Rape*, op. cit., pp. 327–9. Helen Gurley Brown famously advised women to spread semen on the face as part of their skincare regime: see slate.com (7 April 2000). On what Henrietta Moore calls the 'circulatory physics' of breast milk and semen, see her *The Subject of Anthropology* (Cambridge: Polity, 2007) and also Richard Sterba, *Introduction to the Psychoanalytic Theory of Libido* (New York: Nervous and Mental Disease Monographs, 1942). Rubin, see 'Thinking sex: notes for a radical theory of the politics of sexuality', in Carole Vance (ed.), *Pleasure and Danger*, op. cit., pp. 267–319.

p. 161 On male ejaculation in porn, see Steven Strager, 'What men watch when they watch pornography', *Sexuality and Culture*, 7 (2003), pp. 50–61. Lea Seguin et al., 'Consuming ecstasy: representations of male and female orgasm in mainstream pornography', *Journal of Sex Research*, 55 (2018), pp. 348–56.

p. 163 Hamlet, see Gershon Legman, *Oral Techniques in Sexual Intercourse*, op. cit., p. 312; and Gershon Legman, *The Horn Book* (New York: University Books, 1964), pp. 443–4.

p. 165 Mangaia, see Donald Marshall and Robert Suggs, *Human Sexual Behavior*, op. cit., p. 118.

p. 166 Gustave Witkowski, *Tetoniana: Les Seins dans l'Histoire*, 4 vols (Paris: Maloine, 1898–1907).

p. 167 *Blasons*, see Gershon Legman, *Rationale of the Dirty Joke*, vol. 2, op. cit., pp. 704–10; and Nancy Vickers, 'Members only: Marot's anatomical blazons', in David Hillman and Carla Mazzio, *The Body in Parts: Fantasies of Corporeality in Early Modern Europe* (London: Routledge, 1997), pp. 3–22. Jack Litewka, 'The Socialized Penis', *Liberation* magazine (March 1974), pp. 16–24, and repeatedly anthologized.

p. 169 Ovid, *Ars Amatoria*', Book II, lines 683–4. Female ejaculation, see Lowndes Sevely and J. W. Bennett, 'Concerning female ejaculation and the female prostate', *Journal of Sex Research*, 14 (1978), pp. 1–20; and Amy Gilliland, 'Women's experiences of female ejaculation', *Sexuality and Culture*, 13 (2009), pp. 121–34.

p.170 Breast in vagina, see Gregory Zilboorg, 'Some observations on the transformations of instincts', *Psychoanalytic Quarterly*, 7 (1938), pp. 1–24.

p. 171 Mouth and vagina, see Gregory Zilboorg, 'Some observations on the transformations of instincts', op. cit.; Sandor Lorand, 'Contribution to the problem of the vaginal orgasm',

International Journal of Psychoanalysis, 20 (1939), pp. 434–8; Marjorie Brierley, 'Specific determinants in feminine development', op. cit.; and Marie Darrieussecq, *All the Way* (Melbourne: Text Publishing, 2013), p. 197. For Melanie Klein, vaginal activity is initiated by oral frustration: see *The Psychoanalysis of Children* (1932) (London: Hogarth, 1975), pp. 196–7.

p. 172 Vore, see Amy Lykins and James Cantor, 'Vorarephila: a case study in masochism and erotic consumption', *Archives of Sexual Behavior*, 43 (2014), pp. 181–6. Selma Fraiberg, 'Some characteristics of genital arousal and discharge in latency girls', op. cit.; and Phyliss Greenacre, 'Special problems of early female sexual development', *Psychoanalytic Study of the Child*, 5 (1950), pp. 122–38.

p. 174 Sleep at breast, see Daphne and Charles Maurer, *The World of the Newborn* (New York: Basic Books, 1988), p. 95.

p. 175 Lacan on detumescence and the origin of language, see Gisèle Chaboudez, *What Can We Know About Sex?* (London: Routledge, 2022). Talking, see John Gagnon and William Simon, *Sexual Conduct*, op. cit., p. 100. Eighty-nine per cent, see Paul Abramson and Mindy Mechanic, 'Sex and the media: three decades of best-selling books and motion pictures', *Archives of Sexual Behavior*, 12 (1983), pp. 185–206.

p. 176 Consent, see Lori Heise, 'Violence, sexuality and women's lives', in Richard Parker and John Gagnon (eds), *Conceiving Sexuality* (New York: Routledge, 1995), pp. 109–34; Katherine Angel, *Tomorrow Sex Will Be Good Again* (London: Verso, 2021); Jennifer Bennice et al., 'Marital rape: history, research and practice', *Trauma, Violence and Abuse*, 4 (2016), pp. 228–46; and J. Campbell and Peggy Alford, 'The dark consequences of marital rape', *American Journal of Nursing*, 89 (1989), pp. 946–9.

p. 177 On false autonomy and capitalism in sexuality, see Martha McCaughey and Christina French, 'Women's sex-toy parties: technology, orgasm and commodification', *Sexuality and Culture*, 3 (2001), pp. 76–96.

p. 178 Cannon, see Karl and Anne Taylor Fleming, *The First Time*, op. cit., p. 44.

p. 179 Carol Queen points out that even today's 'safe sex' protocols derive in part from the S&M community: see *Real Live Nude Girl*, op. cit., pp. 126–9. Karin Stephen, *'Psychoanalysis and Medicine* (Cambridge: Cambridge University Press, 1933), pp. 142, 152, 157.

p. 180 Saying Yes, see Amber Hollibaugh, *My Dangerous Desires*, op. cit., p. 252.

p. 185 Selective attention, see Seymour Fisher, *Sexual Images of the Self*, op. cit.

p. 186 Rembrandt: this reading was suggested by Wayland Young, *Eros Denied*, op. cit., p. 96.

p. 187 Edrita Fried, *The Ego in Love and Sexuality*, op. cit., p. 150. Ruth Herschberger, *Adam's Rib*, op. cit., p. 102. Bypassing function of sex, see Bernard Apfelbaum, 'Sexual functioning reconsidered', in Robert Gemme and Connie Christine Wheeler, *Progress in Sexology*, op. cit., pp. 93–100.

p. 188 Freud's four, see Jeffrey Moussaieff Masson (ed.), *The Complete Letters of Sigmund Freud to Wilhelm Fliess* (Cambridge, Massachusetts: Harvard University Press, 1985), p. 364. Self-divisions, see Edrita Fried, *The Ego in Love and Sexuality*, op. cit., pp. 135–6, 157–8.

p. 190 Weeing, see Donald Marshall and Robert Suggs (eds), *Human Sexual Behavior*, op. cit.; and Judith Kestenberg, *Children and Parents*, op. cit.

p. 191 This phantasy is clear in de Sade's idea of filling the female genitals to the point of bursting, in *120 Days of Sodom* (Paris: Girodias, 1954), p. 302; and in the horrific example reported by Susan Brownmiller in *Against Our Will: Men, Women and Rape*', op. cit., p. 116.

p. 194 Changes in gender roles re pleasure, see Seymour Fisher, *Sexual Images of the Self*, op. cit., pp. 133–6; Eileen Zurbriggen and Megan Yost, 'Power, desire and pleasure in sexual fantasies', *Journal of Sex Research*, 41 (2004), pp. 288–300; Cindy Meston and David Buss, 'Why humans have sex', *Archives of Sexual Behavior*, 36 (2007), pp. 477–507; and Shira Tarrant, *The Pornography Industry*, op. cit., p. 71.

p. 195 Romance novels and death imagery, see Christine Cabrera and Dana Menard, ' "She exploded into a million pieces": a qualitative and quantitative analysis of orgasms in contemporary romance novels', *Sexuality and Culture*, 17 (2012), pp. 193–212.

p. 196 Seven per cent, see I. S. Arafat and W. L. Cotton, 'Masturbation practices of males and females', *Journal of Sex Research*, 10 (1974), pp. 293–307. Knockout, see Donald Marshall and Robert Suggs (eds), *Human Sexual Behavior*, op. cit., p. 123. Main themes, see Claude Crépault, 'Men's erotic fantasies', *Archives of Sexual Behavior*, 9 (1980), pp. 565–81.

p. 197 Passive imagery, see Claude Crépault, *Les Fantasmes: l'érotisme et la sexualité*, op. cit., p. 151. Rarely against their will, see Nancy Friday, *Men in Love* (New York: Bantam, 1980). Fear, see Theodor Reik, *Masochism in Modern Man* (New York:

Grove Press, 1941); and Claude Crépault, *Les Fantasmes: l'érotisme et la sexualité*, op. cit., p. 178.

p. 198 Freud on splitting, 'A special type of choice of object made by men' (1910), in *The Standard Edition of the Complete Psychological Works of Sigmund Freud*, vol. 11 (London: Hogarth, 1957), pp. 165–175.

p. 200 Antifusion–fusion, see Claude Crépault, *Les Fantasmes: l'érotisme et la sexualité*, op. cit., pp. 46–50, 151.

p. 201 Changes in gender roles re phantasy, see Barbara Hariton and Jerome Singer, 'Women's fantasies during sexual intercourse', *Journal of Counselling and Clinical Psychology*, 42 (1974), pp. 313–22; M. H. Hollender, 'Women's phantasies during sexual intercourse', *Archives of General Psychiatry*, 8 (1962), pp. 86–90; and Theodor Reik, *Sex in Man and Woman* (New York: Bantam, 1967). Sex with animals, see Nancy Friday, *My Secret Garden* (London: Virago, 1975).

p. 202 Coercion fantasies, see Paula Webster, 'Eroticism and taboo', in David Steinberg (ed.), *The Erotic Impulse* (New York: Tarcher, 1992), pp. 129–41; Barbara Hariton, 'The sexual fantasies of women', *Psychology Today*, 6 (1973), pp. 39–44; J. W. Critelli and J. M. Bivona, 'Women's erotic rape fantasies: an evaluation of theory and research', *Journal of Sex Research*, 45 (2008), pp. 57–70; David Strassberg and Lisa Lockerd, 'Force in women's sexual fantasies', *Archives of Sexual Behavior*, 27 (1998), pp. 403–14; Marta Meana, 'Elucidating women's (hetero)sexual desire: definitional challenges and content expansion', op. cit., pp. 104–22; D. Knafo and Y. Jaffe, 'Sexual fantasizing in males and females', *Journal of Research in Personality*, 18 (1984), pp. 451–62; Susan Bond and D. L. Mosher, 'Guided imagery of rape: fantasy, reality, and the willing victim myth', *Journal of Sex Research*, 22 (1986), pp. 162–83; and Eileen Zurbriggen and Megan Yost, 'Power, desire and pleasure in sexual fantasies', op. cit.

p. 203 Rape phantasies as effect of patriarchy, see Susan Brownmiller, *Against Our Will: Men, Women and Rape*, op. cit., p. 359. Rape phantasy as just 'an exaggeration of reality', see Helene Deutsch, *The Psychology of Women*, vol. 1, op. cit., p. 276. Interestingly, despite the social, legal and psychological overinvestment of the male child in many societies, boys are rarely present as sexual figures in female phantasy.

p. 204 Amber Hollibaugh and Cherrie Moraga, 'What we're rollin' around in bed with', *Heresies*, 12 (1981), pp. 58–62.

p. 206 Carole Vance, 'Pleasure and danger: towards a politics of sexuality', in Carole Vance (ed.), *Pleasure and Danger*, op. cit., p. 7. Nancy Friday, *My Secret Garden*, op. cit., p. 280.

p. 207 Cannon, in Karl and Anne Taylor Fleming, *The First Time*, op. cit., p. 48.

p. 210 Wife trading, see William and Jerrye Breedlove, *Swap Clubs* (Los Angeles: Sherbourne, 1964); and Gilbert Bartell, *Group Sex* (New York: New American Library, 1971).

p. 211 Belonging, see Gérard Pommier, 'Le "père incestueux" dans l'hysterie: remarques sur le traumatisme "sexuel"', *La Clinique Lacanienne*, 2 (2000), pp. 195–211; and Judith Kestenberg, *Children and Parents*, op. cit.

p. 212 Rough-sex data, see Shira Tarrant, *The Pornography Industry*, op. cit., p. 95.

p. 213 Claude Crépault, *Les Fantasmes: l'érotisme et la sexualité*, op. cit., p. 156. Robert Stoller, *Sexual Excitement*, op. cit., p. 26. Sadly, much Lacanian psychoanalysis implicitly glorifies female sacrifice, making Medea's act of killing her children the ultimate 'feminine act', but is this any more feminine than, say, not ordering a dessert?

p. 214 Jong, see interview in Karl and Anne Taylor Fleming, *The First Time*, op. cit., p. 128.

p. 216 Note how so much of the print pornography of the seventeenth and eighteenth centuries is cast in the form of dialogues between two women, with a permissive parental figure conveying the message that sex is a legitimate activity which one has every right to enjoy. Licensing, see Sandor Rado, 'An adaptational view of sexual behavior', in Paul Hoch and Joseph Zubin, *Psychosexual Development in Health and Disease*, op. cit., pp. 159–99.

p. 217 Paula Webster, 'Eroticism and taboo', in David Steinberg (ed.), *The Erotic Impulse*, op. cit., pp. 129–41.

p. 220 Sallie Tisdale, *Talk Dirty to Me* (New York: Doubleday, 1994), pp. 68, 98. Horney on ideal partner, see Karen Horney, *Self-Analysis* (New York: Norton, 1942), p. 212.

p. 224 Dating of orgasm, see Judith Kestenberg, *Children and Parents*, op. cit.; and Alfred Kinsey et al., *Sexual Behavior in the Human Male*, op. cit., p. 177. Orgasm movements in infants, see Niles and Michael Newton, 'Psychologic aspects of lactation', *New England Journal of Medicine*, 272 (1967), pp. 1179–967.

p. 225 Alien force, see Judith Kestenberg, *Parents and Children*, op. cit., pp. 4–7, 120. Sandor Felman, 'Anxiety and orgasm', *Psychoanalytic Quarterly*,

---

20 (1951), pp. 528–49. Heaven, see Ellen Vance and Nathaniel Wagner, 'Written descriptions of orgasm: a study of sex differences', *Archives of Sexual Behavior*, 5 (1976), pp. 87–98.

p. 226   Tension states, see Judith Kestenberg, *Children and Parents*, op. cit., pp. 3–24, 75–100, 304–7. Strange enemy, see Ruth Herschberger, *Adam's Rib*, op. cit., p. 96.

p. 228   Use of masturbation, see J. Nydes, 'The magical experience of the masturbation fantasy', *American Journal of Psychotherapy*, 4 (1950), pp. 303–10; and Karin Stephen, *Psychoanalysis and Medicine*, op. cit., p. 186.

p. 229   Unfinished, see Natalie Shainess, 'A re-assessment of feminine sexuality and erotic experience', in Jules Masserman (ed.), *Sexuality of Women* (New York: Grune and Stratton, 1966), pp. 56–74; Mary Jo Sholty et al., 'Female orgasmic experience: a subjective study', op. cit.; and Selma Fraiberg, 'Some characteristics of genital arousal and discharge in latency girls', op. cit.

p. 230   Fear of being too full or emptied out, see Sylvan Keiser, 'On the psychopathology of orgasm', *Psychoanalytic Quarterly*, 16 (1947), pp. 318–29; and Judith Kestenberg, *Children and Parents*, op. cit.

p. 231   Revenge masturbation, see Morton Hunt, *Sexual Behavior in the 1970s*, op. cit., p. 93.

p. 233 Reproach to mother, see Judith Kestenberg, *Children and Parents*, op. cit., pp. 91, 117, 124. Would pop, see Edrita Fried, *The Ego in Love and Sexuality*, op. cit., p. 20.

p. 234 Relief, see Ellen Vance and Nathaniel Wagner, 'Written descriptions of orgasm: a study of sex differences', op. cit. 'Relief' and 'release', see Emily Opperman et al., ' "It feels so good it almost hurts": young adults' experience of orgasm and sexual pleasure', op. cit.

p. 235 Casanova, see Gershon Legman, *The Horn Book*, op. cit., p. 30.

p. 236 Triumph, see Jack Morin, *The Erotic Mind*, op. cit., p. 101.

p. 238 Bernard Apfelbaum, 'On the aetiology of sexual dysfunction', *Journal of Sex and Marital Therapy*, 3 (1977), pp. 50–62. See Freud's comment on this in 'On the universal tendency to debasement in the field of love' (1912), in *The Standard Edition of the Complete Psychological Works of Sigmund Freud*, vol. 11, op. cit., p. 184. Shulamith Firestone, *The Dialectic of Sex*, op. cit., pp. 214–16.

p. 240 Amber Hollibaugh, *My Dangerous Desires*, op. cit, p. 96. Power is heart, ibid., p. 101.

Acknowledgements

My inspirations for this book span the beautiful and the damned: Ruth Herschberger, pioneering writer of the women's movement and gender theorist; Judith Kestenberg, psychoanalyst and student of childhood sexuality; Amber Hollibaugh, LGBTQ+ activist and writer; John Gagnon and William Simon, sociologists of sexuality who were doing Foucault way before Foucault; and Gershon Legman, historian of sexual folklore and practices, self-diagnosed bigot, and author of the most substantial psychoanalytic review of sexuality after Freud. I have learnt so much from these writers, and while not always agreeing with them, their ideas have shaped most of the previous pages.

I developed the themes discussed here in seminars at the Centre for Freudian Analysis and

Research in London, and I'd like to thank everyone there for creating such an open and stimulating space. Special thanks to Julia Carne, Vincent Dachy, Berjanet Jazani, Alexandra Langley, Laura Tarsia, Anne Worthington and Astrid Gessert, who was also kind enough to help me with translations from German. I am grateful to friends and colleagues for their encouragement and input: Josh Appignanesi, Devorah Baum, Anouchka Grose, Hanif Kureishi, Ken Theron and Jay Watts. A big thank you to Stephanie Theobald for her many thoughtful suggestions, criticisms and general knowledge about sex, and to Jamieson Webster for the stimulating Q&A about sexuality that we did for *Spike* magazine.

Thank you to everyone in the sex industry who was kind enough to answer my questions and talk about their experience in such a candid and uncompromising way, illuminating so many aspects of sexual practice. Pat Blackett and Mike Witcombe gave me much-needed help with literature research, and were able to find many items that the web was unable to yield. I am super grateful to Seb for their illuminating comments on the draft and for their insights into the subject. Huge thanks to Clémence Ortega Douville for her generous suggestions and for making me aware of texts and media which resonated with the themes of the book. The unrecognized genius Mary Horlock helped me to formulate many of the key issues discussed, and her support and encouragement were invaluable in drafting the text. Simon Prosser was, as ever, the perfect editor at Hamish Hamilton, and Tracy Bohan at Wylie the maestro agent. A big shout-out to them, and to Hermione Thompson at Hamish Hamilton for her enlightening input, and to Sarah-Jane Forder for her meticulous copy-edit. Finally, thanks to all the analysands who have contributed to this book and whose thoughts on sexuality have oriented, instructed and corrected me.

READ MORE FROM DARIAN LEADER

WHY DO PEOPLE GET ILL?

'Fascinating, important, unusual and timely'

Hanif Kureishi, *Daily Telegraph*

THE NEW BLACK

'There are many self-help books on the market . . . *The New Black* is a book that might actually help'

Independent

WHAT IS MADNESS?

'Engrossing and enlightening . . . Leader is as much a philosopher as a psychoanalyst'

Metro

STRICTLY BIPOLAR

'A timely book. Leader offers illumination and insight; his book is a contribution to a debate but it could also change lives'

Hilary Mantel

HANDS

'An intriguing meditation on how vital our hands are to our understanding of ourselves and our world'

The Times

WHY CAN'T WE SLEEP?

'Persuasive, absorbing and refreshingly sane . . . Leader points the way to a richer and more humane understanding of our problems with sleep'

Guardian